THE WISEMAN MASSACRE

The History of the
Henson and Pheobe Wiseman Family

TO:
Dorothy

LOUISE GUY

7/14/11

Louise R. Guy

First printing, May 2002
Second printing, September 2003

Printed in the United States of America
PINE HILL PRESS
4000 West 57th Street
Sioux Falls, S.D. 57106

Introduction

In the year 2001, several of us former St. James parishioners (and others) decided to start the St. James Marketplace. A place where us farmers and farm wives could bring together our farm made items and market them and hopefully make some extra money in our tight economy. I knew that I could sell garden items and baked items, but I also knew, that the income from that wasn't going to pay for my time, cost of materials, gas etc. It occurred to me, I'm married to a Wiseman descendant. Louis and our children are a part of Henson Wiseman's legacy. Thus, I decided to compile a book about the Wiseman Massacre.

With much skepticism I began my new challenge. In researching this, I have come across many articles, each with a different twist. So I decided to include most of them making it more interesting. So many different stories made it hard to nail down the cold hard facts about the massacre, some I'll probably never know.

I hope you enjoy this book. It's been a learning experience for me and I hope it is for you too.

Louise Guy

Acknowledgments

Thank You to everyone who helped in any way with this book. Your time and effort was very much appreciated. Thank you to, in no certain order, Louis Guy, Ray and Marjorie Guy, my "push and shove" group of Violet Pinkelman, Vicky Koch, Mary Rose Pinkelman and Jeanette Pinkelman. Karen Guy, Martha Masgai, Mary Ann Hoebelheinrich, Carol Tramp, Joan Burney, B. Paul Chicoine, Sally McCluskey, Danny Liska, SS. Philip & James History Committee, Cedar County News, Yankton Press & Dakotan, Larry Swanson and Nebraska Game and Parks.

Table of Contents

Other sources of reading material about the Wiseman Massacre:

Cedar County Who's Who in Nebraska, 1940
History of Cedar County by J. Mike McCoy
History of Cedar County, Nebraska by Twila Anderson
Pioneer Families of Cedar County

A Brief History

Of The

MASSACRE

Of The

Wiseman Children

Which Occurred in the North Part of Cedar
County, Nebraska, July 23, 1863.

The following letter was written to the U.S. Congress, by Henson Wiseman in 1894, thirty two years after the massacre. Henson wrote this letter, asking for settlement of his claim, which was restitution for the items stolen by the Indians at the time of the massacre. And it may have also included the $600 in expenses that he incurred going back to West Virginia to live for one year. His claim was never settled, even after trying three times.

On the 5th day of November, 1817, in Harrison county, West Virginia, I, the subscriber, was born.

In 1838 I was married at Parkersburg, W. Va., to Pheobe Ann Cross. In the year 1839 I emigrated westward with my wife and at Burlington, Iowa, I found a home, where I remained for a number of years; afterwards removing to Fort Des Moines, Iowa. During all this time, by dint of perseverance, hard and incessant toil, at my trade (carpentering), and other work when I could not find employment at my trade, I accumulated a little money and some property.

In 1856 I removed from Des Moines to Sioux City, Iowa, where I found employment at my trade, and am accredited with roofing the first house, which was covered with shingles, in that town.

In 1857 I removed from Sioux City, Iowa, to Cedar county, Nebraska, and settled upon a piece of land under the "Squatter law" (the land not being surveyed at that time) where I have resided, principally, until the present time, acquiring title to my land by United States Patent after the land was surveyed and placed upon the market by the government.

During the time of my residence in Iowa there were born to me eight children, two of whom died and were buried in that state. When I came to Nebraska I had six children, five boys and one girl. One of the boys, Benjamin F., died in 1859. His was the first natural death in Cedar county, Neb. In the same year another son was born, making the number of my children six -- five of whom were at home at the time of the happening of the tragical events hereinafter narrated, one of said children (John) being in the U. S. army fighting for his country, and far away from home. The five remaining being the same that were massacred, as hereinafter mentioned.

*In 1863 the population of the county did not exceed 275, including about 50 citizens who had enlisted in Comp. I, 2d Neb. Cav., raised for the purpose of defending the frontier settlements against Indians. Of this number were " * Henson Wiseman." (See The Western Historical Co.'s History of Nebraska, 1882, page 528.)*

In October 1862, the government called for a company of cavalry, second regiment. I enlisted in company "I" as I believed the government needed all possible help, and to get protection to life and property. I should give a helping hand. I left my family in good condition and took a soldier's fare and outfit at the age of forty-five, supposing for home guards, to be to the order of the government used as scouts in Nebraska, in our then frontier settlements, then exposed to savage butchery.

We were ordered away to join Sully's regiment in Dakota; the whole regiment. I supposed a regiment would take our place when we left, but not a soldier ever came till the savages went at their usual deeds of destruction. If I had known the government or counsel, of savage warfare so ignorant, I would have sent my family away when I left.

The company was called together fifty miles away from home, at Dakota City, Nebraska, under John Taffe, then captain. I remained from home all winter. During the month of June, or the last of May, I obtained a furlough to go and see my family before starting with the expedition. I told my wife and children where we were going, and they all cried and said, "The Indians will kill us if we stay here and you leave us." I told them that other soldiers would come as soon as we were gone. Now my children were put to a wretched death by the ignorance of the government; (that was the last I ever saw of them) anyone there of knowledge would say the Indians would come in behind; I knew this and said so, (if given a chance) to many of my comrades. About thirty days from the time I left home, while at Crow Creek, two hundred miles off, this bloody deed was done, and done by the Yankton and Santee Sioux on the 23rd day of July, 1863, between nine and ten o'clock of said day.

My wife was not at home at this time, but was at Yankton buying something for the family, or she too would have shared the same fate as the rest of the family. They killed the family for plunder, as one of them was seen at Crow agency wearing my wife's new shoes. My wife, the mother of these five children, returned home in the evening, and as soon as she got to the door seeing an Indian lying on the floor and blood on the door, fled around the house and there saw one boy lying on his back dead. On seeing this she was perfectly horrified, and convinced of the condition of the rest. She fled as soon as possible out of sight to the settlement of St. James, three miles away, leaving all roads and going through high weeds and brush all dripping wet with rain, a heavy rain having fallen only two hours before. What kind of feelings for a female in her condition! Is this protection, I ask? The few inhabitants now thrown into excitement, dared not go the same night to see; going the next day nine miles around on the open prairie, found three dead and two nearly so. The youngest boy, aged five years could tell, "the Indians scared him," was all he ever said; he was stabbed under the left arm and lived three days. The girl fifteen years of age, as savages always do, bore savage infamy until they were satisfied; a cartridge put in her mouth, was set on fire, tearing out her teeth; then passing an arrow through her birth and out at the top of each hip; left her in that condition for dead; she was alive and lived five days; never spoke a word but looked wildly around to anyone that came in her sight. The other three were dead; one boy, aged eight years, was found out doors shot through with a ball and three buck-shot; all the rest were in the house. The next boy, aged thirteen years, was stabbed twice in the left side. The oldest boy, aged seventeen, had his head and arms all broken and mashed, his gun, clutched in his hands, showed an overhand fight and was empty. There were four guns in the house; two the Indians took and two they left. There were several letters written to me, mailed every week, but I never received one of them; some one got my mail to keep down a mutiny in the regiment. The same Indians gave the news at Crow agency, wearing my wife's shoes, eight days before the news reached us that some family in Cedar county had been butchered by Indians. When the report reached me that it was my family, I was guarding some horses grazing two miles from camp. About daylight I mounted my horse and went to camp, knowing what was before me, (200 miles.) I left without anything to eat, as I could get nothing until I reached Fort Randall, one hundred miles away. I traveled night and day until I reached home, stopping at the Fort two hours to get something to eat and rest my horse; there the commander of the post showed his authority. I showed fight and sixty rounds of cartridges, and told him that I was the commander of that Fort and would shoot him on the spot; that I was not a deserter but had been deserted. A soldier came up and told the commander who I was, and said to me, "Don't shoot him;" that I was welcome to all I wanted. In twenty minutes Company "A" of my own regiment, stationed there, came to me and told me to stay at the Fort as long as I wished, and leave when I was ready.

They gave me all I wanted. I went to Yankton reserve that night and learned from an Indian interpreter all I wanted. I wrote a letter to my colonel "to keep all the boys and fight the Indians when found, that they had gone up James river with what they had taken from me, and I would take care of myself and northeastern Nebraska."

I reached Yankton the next day at nine o'clock, sick, and reported to Capt. Tripp's company on the sick list. There I learned that my wife had been waiting for me a week, but had left for Sioux City and was nearly insane. I went to St. James, Nebraska to rest a few days. I stayed there five days not knowing where my wife had gone. I trembled all over with fatigue and anger when the neighbors were telling me about the massacre. Savages were strolling all around there. I had been to my own house. I saw all I wanted as there was blood all over the house floor, dried down twenty-five days. I started one evening after dark for Sioux City to look for my wife. I met her the 28th day of August on the Aoway creek coming home. She wailed and cried and tried to tell her grief but could not, and it was a year before she could tell it all. We returned to St. James the same day, and began at once to prepare some place in which to live. We had no home, nothing to live on, no clothing except what we had on our backs, which we had worn for many weeks. I knew we were in a hard climate and a hard place. Many is the time my poor wife would moan in her sleep and call for her children. I would then awake her, and then she would moan and bewail the sad fate of her children and would finally sob herself to sleep. I could not sleep contented for three years.

On the 8th day of March * * * my wife gave birth to a boy baby, which was born restless under great trouble, and for two years he would cry himself to sleep and wake up crying, and now, although thirty-two years have passed, is hard to reconcile in many ways, and is entirely helpless. My wife bearing all this trouble and being nearly deranged, I took her east to see former friends and where she could feel more safe. I remained east one year, which cost me six hundred dollars and much trouble in many ways. Before I got back I spent all the money I had. Now, to begin anew, I had to pay taxes on property the Indians took. This was all done thirty-two years ago. I sent to the United States congress a bill with affidavits of property, time and money lost, fifty dollars costs. Congress did not look at it. Ten years go by and I send in a petition signed by three governors, of two states and one territory. Senator Hitchcock was then in congress and he presented the bill which many citizens had signed, and congress refused to settle it. Now to a candid world. If I should treat one of my neighbors as I have been treated by the government, I would have been put out of sight long ago. Thirty-two years have passed. I did not live on government land nor on the Indian's hunting ground. But forced in old age to hard labor; my life made miserable; my family buried in blood, dirt and rags, like so many dogs; their mother not able to see them to their resting place. I received an honorable discharge from the army, but not from dread of duty. Those Indians stole from me for four years after all this. I was on my guard and was shot at.

I wore a Colt's revolver for five years, night and day, and during the day I spent the time working for my bread, and at night examining the country for miles around to be sure that no Indians would be in waiting at dawn of day, as I knew their intentions were to kill me. I employed a young man for one year to act as scout for me, at $25 per month.

I now make one more appeal to congress that my claim may be settled according to the invoice filed in congress years ago. (See invoice record of Dakota county, Nebraska.) I now appeal to law and justice. Paddock and Saunders having failed, and senator Hitchcock having died while the matter was pending in congress. Will the representatives and senators from Nebraska, as well as all members of congress, do for their humble servant what is just? I, an American citizen 77 years old, beg an immediate settlement.

HENSON WISEMAN

The Unveiling

Of The

Wiseman Monument

June 6th, 1926

WISEMAN MEMORIAL DEDICATED SOON

JOHN WISEMAN, SON OF HENSON, WILL UNVEIL MONUMENT

John Wiseman, son of Henson Wiseman, whose children were massacred by the Indians, will unveil the monument which the women of the Wynot Country Club have purchased as a memorial to the oldest settler of Cedar County. The unveiling and dedicatory services will be held about the 1st of June.

The monument will be placed on the spot where the children were massacred and will have the names and ages of the children and those of Mr. and Mrs. Wiseman.

Being hewn of gray granite the monument will have a rough surface except for the face on which the inscriptions will be placed. It is seven feet high, three and one half feet wide and 18 inches thick, weighs 5,200 pounds and will cost $500.00. Around the monument will be placed at a distance of about four feet an iron fence set in a concrete base and a concrete walk will lead to the road. Behind the monument stand two trees a locust and cottonwood which Henson Wiseman planted on his homestead. These will be safeguarded as living monuments. The plot is 35 feet wide and 130 feet long and was donated by Theodore Beste of Hartington who owns the land on which the monument is being erected.

Mrs. J G Campbell, who is the president of the country club at Wynot, Mrs. H.L. Sprinkle, Mrs. J. Warnock, Mrs. H.A. McCormick Sr., Mrs. Ben Heil, Mrs. G.A. Snowe, Mrs. Ludwig Olson, Mrs. Geo Gowery, and Mrs. Tess Ferber were in Hartington Wednesday soliciting donations for the memorial and were entertained for supper at the home of Mrs. Tom Denny.

NOTE: THE WYNOT TRIBUNE CEASED OPERATIONS IN THE LATE 1930s.

WISEMAN MEMORIAL DEDICATION SUNDAY

MRS. LAURA LAWSON OF WYNOT WILL UNVEIL MONUMENT

Mrs. Laura Lawson of Wynot, only living child of Henson Wiseman will unveil the monument erected in honor of the memory of the Wiseman children who were massacred by the Indians in 1863 and of the parents who helped to build up the county. The dedicatory services will begin at 2 o'clock Sunday afternoon four and one half miles northeast of Wynot, just below the bluff.

Addison E. Sheldon, secretary of the Nebraska Historical Society of Lincoln will deliver the address. Mr. Sheldon is an authority on the early development of the state and will have a real message to give. Invocation will be asked by Rev. M.E. Coltrane of Wynot. Mrs. J.G. Campbell president of the country club of Wynot thru whose leadership the monument has been secured, will give a short address of welcome. Short talks will also be given by George Beste of Hartington, N.E. Osthant and Rev. D.M. McIntosh. There will be special musical numbers and two bands will furnish several concerts during the afternoon and evening.

Mrs. Campbell first conceived the idea of erecting a monument on the spot where the Wiseman children were massacred in 1924. The other members of the country club eagerly took up the task and have worked earnestly since. Mrs. G.W. Butler is vice-president of the organization, Mrs. George Gowery is secretary, and Mrs. R.H. Baugous, treasurer. The club was organized in 1921 and Mrs. Campbell has been president since its organization.

The land on which the monument has been placed was donated for that purpose by Theodore Beste of Hartington. Mr. Beste was a pioneer resident of Brookey Bottom with the Wiseman family and was a personal friend for many years. Later he served the county very ably as county commissioner.

The monument cost $600, half of which was raised by the club women and the other half by subscriptions. It is chiseled out of gray marble and has a rough surface except the face on which the names of the massacred children and their parents will be inscribed.

This memorial will mark the spot where in the summer of 1863 five of the children of Mr. and Mrs. Henson Wiseman were massacred while the mother was in Yankton for supplies and Mr. Wiseman was with the US army on the Dakota Frontier. The oldest son, John, was wearing the Blue in the Union army in the south. It was to have been his honor to unveil the monument, but death claimed him about two months ago. A sister, Mrs. Laura Lawson of Wynot born after the tragedy, will now be given the honor.

Many folks from all over the county and the surrounding territory as well plan to attend the services Sunday afternoon. For those who wish to picnic for the day there are many lovely spots in the vacinity where the day may be enjoyably spent.

Unveiling Wiseman Monument

MEMORIAL IS CONCEIVED AND ERECTED BY THE LADIES OF THE COUNTRY CLUB.

The monument marking the scene of the Wiseman massacre, which occurred on July 23, 1863, will be unveiled with appropriate program and addresses on Sunday afternoon, June 6, 1926, at 2:30 o'clock.

The monument, purchased and erected through the efforts of the Country club and assisted by citizens of every part of Cedar county and other citizens of the state, was erected on the spot just opposite the Brockey bottom school house this week. The plot of land is as near the site of the massacre as it is possible to locate it. It is on the Theodore Beste farm and the grounds, sufficient for the monument and a smnall park in connection, was leased by Mr. Beste for a period of 99 years.

The monument is seven feet high and three feet wide and weighs 5200 pounds. It is erected on a neat concrete foundation. A neat iron fence will be erected around the monument and the little park will be enclosed with a woven wire fence to protect the grounds.

PROGRAM OF UNVEILING.

The following program for the unveiling has been arranged by Mrs. J. G. Campbell, president, with the assistance of the other members of the club, and will be given as stated above on Sunday, June 6th, at 2:30 p. m., 1926

Song—America -- Audience
Invocation ------------------------------- Rev. M. E. Coltrane
Selection -------------------------------- Double Quartet
Address by the President -------------------- Mrs. J. G. Campbell
Five Minute Talks -------------------- Geo. Beste, S. C. Oathout
Selection -- Wynot Band
Five Minute Talks ------ Rev. D. M. McIntosh, Dr. F. O. Robinson
Selection ----------------------------------- Double Quartet
Memorial Address ---------------------- Dr. Addison E. Sheldon
        Secretary Nebraska Historical Society, Lincoln.
Unveiling of Monument ---------------------- Mrs. L. Lawson

The Obert band will also be present and give a concert while the crowd is assembling.

The ladies have arranged to receive and care for a large crowd. There will be ample parking space for automobiles within a short distance of the site of the program. No lunch will be esrved, but those wishing to bring picnic dinners or suppers will find many very fine places for enjoying a picnic and are cordially welcome to come.

All papers concerning the Wiseman massacre and data in connection with the same are being placed in a steel box at the base of the monument.

As this part of Cedar county is one of the most beautiful spots in Nebraska, all should avail themselves of the opportunity to attend this unveiling and enjoy a drive in one of our little known beauty spots.

CEDAR COUNTY NEWS JUNE 10, 1926

WISEMAN MONUMENT UNVEILED SUNDAY

NEARLY 1,500 PEOPLE ATTENDED CEREMONIES AT HISTORICAL SPOT

In spite of an extremely windy Sunday approximately 1,500 people attended the dedication and unveiling of the Wiseman memorial on the spot four miles northeast of Wynot where the Wiseman children were massacred by the Santee Sioux and Yankton Indians in the summer of 1863. Mrs. Laura Lawson, the only living child of Henson Wiseman unveiled the statue which the women of the Wynot Country club have built on the memorable place.

At two o'clock the program was opened by invocation asked by Rev. M.E. Coltrane of Wynot. Mrs. J.G. Campbell, president of the Country club gave the opening address and Addison E. Sheldon secretary of the Nebraska Historical Society delivered the address of the day. Others who spoke are George Beste, P.F. O'Gara, of Hartington, S.C. Oathaut and Rev. D.M. McIntosh. Special music had been provided for the afternoon and two bands furnished music throughout the day.

The names of the Wiseman family are inscribed on the face of the monument and those members of the Country club on the back of the stone.

The monument rests on the spot where the Wiseman children were killed in the humble cabin built by their father, on the homestead taken by Henson Wiseman. It is situated on a knoll facing the Missouri River and overlooking the surrounding country. The natural beauty of the spot gives many Cedar county residents the hope that it may be made into a state park, and preserved as one of the historical places in Nebraska.

Early History of Cedar County and the Northwest as told at the Henson Wiseman Memorial Unveiling

Address by Hon. Addison E. Sheldon,
Secretary of Nebraska Historical Society

In every place and every period of the three hundred years conflict between the white man and Indian for possession of the North American continent there has been some outstanding spot marking the high point of the conflict for that region. Deerfield, Mass. is one such spot, Wyoming Valley, Pennsylvania is another, Tippecanoe Battlefield, Indiana, is another, Bad Axe, Wisconsin is another. Wounded Knee, South Dakota, was the last battlefield between the White race and Red race and is altogether likely to be the last. It was the fortune of that part of the White race belonging to my family and bearing my name to have a leading part in the Deerfield massacre, February 29, 1704. The Sheldon house was the last defense captured by the Indians in that massacre. It was my fortune to help bury the dead on the Wounded Knee battlefield on December 29, 1890, so that the experience of my family covers the entire period of conflict between these two races on this continent and I may therefore speak with more than usual personal interest of that conflict and of the episode therein which we commemorate today.

The white settlement of northeastern Nebraska was not accompanied by Indian War. It was a peaceful, trading contact. The first white men in this region were French furtraders, coming here about the year 1704. One of the earliest of them was named Laurain. They followed the Mississippi from the Illinois settlements a little below the present city of St. Louis to its junction with the Missouri. They followed the Missouri, no one knows just how far, for these frontiersmen carried no instruments to make astronomical observations and reported no degrees of latitude or longitude where they arrived. They do report, however, the great bend of the Big Muddy river at the present site of Sioux City. They reported the names of the Indian tribes whom they found at that bend of the Missouri, — the chief tribes being the Yankton Sioux on the north and east of the Missouri, the Ponca or Ponca Nation on the south and west near the mouth of the Niobrara and Maha or Omaha on both sides of the Missouri from the vicinity of Bow river and Sioux river around the big bend of the Missouri and southward. The names of these tribes appear upon maps in Europe more than 200 years ago and the characteristics of the tribes were described by these early traders. Two of these traders, — James Mackay and Zenon Trudeau — at different times in the decade between 1790 and 1800 spent many months in this region. They made explorations and maps and they wrote in detail the story of their life with these Indian tribes. So that the definite recorded history of the Indians at the big bend of the Missouri begins about 1794, and that year should be through all future ages, for dwellers on these plains, similar in its reckoning to that of 1492 for the North American Continent. Trudeau's letters have been found in the last twenty years and have been translated from French into English. They give us the first accurate picture from personal contact with the great chief Blackbird who had become famous by the word of mouth reports from the later settlers around the big westward bend of the Missouri river.

The years 1862, 1863, 1864 were bloody years in border warfare on the western frontier. On the 17th of August, 1862, the great massacre along the Minnesota river led by Little Crow at the head of a band of warriors drawn from the Sioux tribes of that region startled the entire frontier. Nearly a thousand settlers, men, women and children, were tortured and murdered in the most shocking ways known to all the annals of Indian warfare. And these same Indians had been for years visitors at the pioneer cabins of white settlers throughout the entire region. My father's family settled in southern Minnesota in 1856 and the earliest tales of my childhood were the blood curdling recitals of the atrocities of the Sioux only a few miles to the west of the family home. Then followed the siege of Fort Ridgely by the Indians, their defeat, the gathering of white forces under General Sully, the defeat of the Sioux warriors at Birch Coulee and driving of the hostile Sioux out of Minnesota into the great unknown region between the Missouri river and the Minnesota valley. Runners from the hostile Sioux went out to every Indian tribe and nation between the Rocky Mountains and the Mississippi river, calling upon their kinsmen everywhere to forget their feuds and join in one more effort to drive the white man from the Indian lands and gain back the graves of their fathers. These runners were aided by emissaries of the rebel states of the south. It was everywhere made plain that the white men in the great Mississippi valley were fighting each other, that thousands of white men were being killed and that the war might go on for many years. This was the great opportunity long awaited by the Indians of the west. The white soldiers had been largely withdrawn from the frontier and the united Indian tribes might now recover their old hunting grounds and regain possession of their lands.

A great council of the Indian tribes of the plains and mountains was held in 1863 on Horse Creek in Nebraska, and after days of counseling and feasting, war against the whites was declared along the frontier, the tomahawk and scalping knife were sharpened and war signals passed swiftly from the Red river of the north to the distant Rio Grande, making for the next two years one continuos battle line of Red Warriors across two thousand miles of frontier.

In October, 1862, the call came to Nebraska to organize a new regiment to fight hostile Indians and protect the white settlements. The First Nebraska had already gone south under General Thayer, the Curtis Horse of Iowa and several other commands had been largely recruited from Nebraska settlers. Now the call came for yet another regiment from the thin and scattered frontier settlements. Robert W. Furnas, editor of the Brownville Advertiser and the Nebraska Farmer, laid down his pen and printer's composing stick and started to organize the new regiment. Companies were quickly enlisted at Falls City, at Brownville, at Omaha, and as far north as Dakota City. Guns and ammunition, also uniforms were sent up the Missouri river and the active work of drilling and training the farmer of the frontier for the soldier life began.

In Company I of the Second Nebraska cavalry there enlisted on October 28, 1862, Henson Wiseman. I have here the original enlistment record in the company Descriptive book from which I read: "Age, 44; Height, 6 ft; Complexion, dark; Eyes, dark; Hair, black; Born, Harrison, Virginia; Occupation, farmer; Enlisted at Dakota City, by Captain John Taffee; Term of enlistment, nine months.

This book you will notice has seen some campaigning itself. Of all the original records of the Second Nebraska Cavalry this original book shows the hardest experience.

Henson Wiseman became a settler in Nebraska near St. James in Cedar county in 1857 as given by his own statement. He built a log cabin near a spring where there was abundance of timber and brought to that log cabin his wife (Phoebe Ann Cross) whom he married in 1838 at Parkersburg, West Va., and six children, five boys and one girl. At the time there were in Cedar county a total of not to exceed ten families, perhaps fifty people, all of whom moved here about the same time that Henson Wiseman located. The land was not surveyed by the United States. The zealous representative of the region in the territorial legislature caused an act to be passed creating Cedar county which was signed by Governor Izard, February 12, 1857. The principal industry in all Cedar county was cutting cord wood for Missouri river steam boats. Thirty or forty steamboats passed up and down the river each summer making market at various landings for the wood necessary to boil the muddy Missouri and make enough steam pressure to stem its current. In the very year that Henson Wiseman and the little handful of families with him located in Cedar county came the panic of 1857. Most of the little money which circulated along the Missouri river was paper currency of wild cat banks. It lost at once even the pretense of exchange value. Mark Twain's story illustrates the point.

A steamboat captain on his way up the Missouri hailed a typical frontiersman standing near a pile of cord wood on the river bank, the following dialogue takes place:

"What kind of wood have you got there?" "Cord wood." "How long has it been cut?" "Four feet long." "What's the price?" "What kind of money have you?" "Fontenelle Bank." "I'll trade cord for cord."

But game was abundant. A frontiersman with a good gun could get meat. A little patch of clearing gave vegetables and sometimes a little corn. Ft. Randall about eighty miles up the river, had a military garrison and a few traders where skins and furs could be swapped for frontier necessities. An occasional trip thru the woods or down the river to Sioux City put the settler at least in contact with the primitive needs of life, powder and lead, bacon, coffee, tobacco and sometimes flour. Such was pioneer life in Northeastern Nebraska from 1857 until the day in October, 1862, when Henson Wiseman took the oath as a soldier of the United States to obey orders as a private in the Second Nebraska Cavalry.

A few weeks after Henson Wiseman put on the uniform of a United States soldier his regiment was ordered north into Dakota to take part in Sully's campaign against the hostile Sioux. He obtained a furlough of a few days about the first of June 1863 and came home to the log cabin in Bow Valley to say good-bye to his wife and children. They clung to him saying, "The Indians will kill us if you leave us and march away with your regiment." But he answered like a soldier rather than a husband and father and said, "No, the government will protect you. Other troops will guard the river from Ft. Randall, while we march North." So they marched. The Second Nebraska Cavalry and the Sixth Iowa crossed South Dakota, an unbroken wilderness, into the present North Dakota, near Pollack, and along Long Lake in Burleigh county on to White Hill, where on September 3, 1863, was fought the battle that broke the power and the will to war of the Sioux, — ending the campaign. Fifty-eight of the Second Nebraska Cavalry were killed and wounded in this battle for our regiment bore the brunt of the fight.

Before the battle of White Stone Hill was fought, in August, Henson Wiseman was doing duty as a soldier with his regiment near Crow Creek Agency on the Missouri river. Some Indians came to Crow Creek Agency bringing with them plunder from settlers' homes. In some way Henson Wiseman saw some of the plunder, a pair of shoes. It turned the blood in his veins, first to ice, then to hot steam, for he recognized the shoes as belonging to his own family.

Henson Wiseman had taken an oath to obey orders as a soldier in the army of the United States. He was on duty guarding horses. He mounted his own horse swung his rifle across his shoulder, left his guard duty and rode 100 miles across the naked wilderness to Fort Randall. He did not report to his Commanding Officer and ask for leave of absence. He knew, as every soldier knows, how long it takes to tie red tape around military headquarters. He was a soldier, I say. But he was more a frontiersman even than he was a soldier. A frontiersman learns to be his own commander. He must be or he would not survive on the frontier. Henson Wiseman had been on the frontier from the mountains of Virginia to the shores of the Missouri. He had served more years in the army of the American pioneer than he had served weeks in the Second Nebraska Cavalry.

Henson Wiseman was more than a frontiersman. He was a frontier husband and father. That means a great deal more than a husband and a father in civilized life. The frontier father knows that upon his efforts, his courage, his skill, his devotion, depends from day to day the honor and the life of the little family he has undertaken to rear. Out on the naked prairie, or in the solitary solitude of the forest stands a frontiersman's home. Sometimes a neighbor in sight, sometimes none for weeks and months. All the wild animals and wild men about them. The family learns to live the life, to rely upon itself, to be ready for any danger and emergency. But the man of the family learns from the day that he hears the cry of the first baby in his house that the existence of the group depends on him. He must live up to that obligation if the frontier is not to fail, if the frontiersman picket line is not to be driven back.

So Henson Wiseman, frontiersman, husband and father rode away from the company roll call, from the keen eye of the First Sergeant, rode away from his regiment, rode, without rations, toward his home in the woods in the valley of the Bow river.

"A. W. O. L." — absent without leave — a serious charge to stand against a soldier. Overseas, in France, I was told during the World War that at one time forty thousand American soldiers were A. W. O. L. But that was after the 11th day of November, 1918. I loaned two of those fellows money to get out of Paris and return to their command. They made their defense to me during the negotiation for the loan. I understood it before they told me. The war was over. They knew it. There was nothing more for them to do as soldiers. They knew that, after some weeks and months, they would be loaded in box cars bearing the familiar legend, "8 Cheveaux & Hommes", and shipped like so many live stock to some sea port, shoved into the steerage deck of a trans-Atlantic steamer and shiver and swim in the ocean spray all the way across the Atlantic to reach America. And those American dough-boys resolved that they were going to see something of Europe besides the stinking trenches and broken battlefields. They knew the risk and they cheerfully accepted it. They would rather get back to a little of the old freedom which they knew as free born American citizens and see a little of Europe while dodging the M. P.'s than to stay in camp and wait for the military machine finally to grind out the order for home. Some of the bravest men who did some of the hardest fighting overseas took their chance and went A. W. O. L.

And here was Henson Wiseman in August, 1863, riding without rations, across the vacant grass land of Dakota and Nebraska A. W. O. L., bound for home. Burning up the trail under his horse's feet to get home. What did he care for military orders and court-martial. There was one frontier Nebraska home which was his chief business in life to protect and he was going there. So he rode the first 100 miles into Fort Randall. And the military guard and the commanding officer there naturally demanded his pass. "To hell with a pass." He defied the commander and the military law of the United States, and the guard house and court martial, and he rode down the river bank and headed for the log cabin in the woods in Cedar county, Nebraska.

It is a splendid thing to be a soldier, and obey orders, and to take the drill and discipline, and to become a part of the military machine, for it takes military machines to win battles in the great wars of our time. But there are bigger and better things than being a soldier, and obeying orders, and becoming an efficient unit in the big military machine in time of national danger. And one of those bigger and better things is being a free American citizen, an intelligent, independent soul, a defender of one's home and in knowing when to obey orders and when to defy them. Some of the greatest victories of the human race on the battlefield, in the forum, on the frontier, in the hearts of men and in the sight of God, have been won by those big enough and brave enough to disobey orders and to strike straight through the underbrush of human rules and regulations for the protection of the main purpose of life.

And that is what Henson Wiseman, soldier, frontiersman, husband and father was doing in August, 1863, when he rode away from his regiment toward his log cabin home, where he ought to have been in the Second Nebraska Cavalry.

I shall not here relate all the record of July 23, 1863 at the Wiseman log cabin on the Bow river in Cedar county, Nebraska. It is a story like a thousand similar stories of the conflict between the White and Red man across this continent. I shall mention the murder and torture of the five Wiseman children left alone in their log cabin on that July day while the mother walked miles across the prairie to the little village of St. Helena on the bank of the Missouri river to get supplies for the little family. Why did not the mother remain at home that day and perhaps add another to the victims? Every pioneer knows why. The children of the pioneer homes learn to live alone for hours and even days while father and mother are gone on the errands of existence. I have ridden up myself, many times, to a frontier log cabin or sod house in Nebraska and seen a little bunch of tow-heads, like startled rabbits, dodge into a corn field or peer from around the corral at the stranger. Frontier children have had to learn to take their chance alone many times in the march of the White race across the continent. Some of them survived and some perished. But the survivors pushed on and the line was carried to its objective like a line of soldiers crossing broken ground under machine gun fire.

In that group of Wiseman children was a boy of 17, found with a gun clutched in his hands, his head and arms broken. There was a girl of sixteen, tortured and abused, mutilated and yet living for five days after the Indian assault. There was a boy of 13, stabbed in the left side and lying dead. There was a boy of eight shot through with a bullet and three buckshot, and there was the youngest boy five years old stabbed under the left arm, living three days and all that he could say before he died was "The Indians scared me."

So the mother came back from her tramp on foot of twenty-five miles and found in the twilight of that July day what had been her home and her dead and dying children. There was an Indian lying on the floor and she fled in fright through the darkness to find help. She fled avoiding the trail for fear of discovery. Thru the grass and the trees and the brush and over broken ground she fled, with the rain falling about her, to the nearest settlement of St. James and the settlers there waited until daylight before they dared risk the journey to the log cabin, where they found the Indians all gone and only the dead and dying children.

So they buried the children and kept the crazed mother for a few days until she broke away from the settlement to reach Sioux City. No one knew exactly where she was for some days.

And in August, a month after the massacre, Henson Wiseman reached the end of his journey and found the broken and empty cabin, with the floor covered with blood, and the stories of the settlers and finally on August 28, as he tells us found his wife on Aowa Creek, on her way back to the cabin which one time had been home. So the wife of Henson Wiseman tried to tell him the story, but she told it with tears instead of words. Her grief

was too great to relate. It was more than a year, so Henson Wiseman tells us, before his wife could tell it bit by bit in all its bitterness. But she moaned and sobbed in her sleep for the children that were gone.

They say that Henson Wiseman was a changed man from the day he rode away from the army to the end of his life. It might well be true. From the day he found his broken home he swore enmity to the Indian race. The Nebraska State Historical Society was presented at its meeting last January with the rifle of Henson Wiseman at the hands of Judge Radke of Tecumseh. Cedar county citizens have told me that Henson Wiseman carried his rifle with him through the years; that he was always ready at the sight of an Indian to level the loaded rifle and fire. I am not sure how absolutely true this tradition may be. I cannot commend it in Henson Wiseman whether true or not. I cannot commend it as I commend his disobeying orders and riding away from his regiment. For I know, if true, it carries no such glory and no such insignia of justice as risking ones life in defiance of the provost guard and military commander at Fort Randall. For it must always be said after doing full justice to the dying and the suffering of the white frontiersman, that the Indian has suffered as much injustice at the hands of the White man as the White man has at the hands of the Red man. I have seen with my own eyes on the battlefield of Wounded Knee Indian babies torn with bullets and burned with the fires of falling teepees. And I know no massacre of white people, which has been matched in its main features, by some of the massacres of Indians at the hands of White men. I know, moreover, by more than fifty years of life in Nebraska; by the playmates of my childhood who were Pawnee Indians; by the companions of my later manhood who were Sioux and Cheyenne and Omaha; that some of the finest qualities of the human race have been exhibited before me in the Indian peoples of the plains.

War makes beasts of men. Ask some of the conscientious, sensitive souls, who saw fighting overseas what they have witnessed of the cruelties of men set at the task of killing each other; or ask some of the fast disappearing men who wore the blue in the

Civil War and receive from them, as I have received, some of the stories of the Civil War, when we Americans fought against each other. An Indian is nearer by nature and training to the wild animal than the White man and, by the same reasoning, an Indian warrior is more of a wild beast than a White warrior. Indian atrocities upon the living and dead exceed those of White men engaged in the similar business of killing. But it is as bad to hold one Indian responsible for the atrocities of another Indian as to hold one citizen of Chicago — responsible for the devilish deeds of another citizen of Chicago. So I hope that the tradition of Henson Wiseman shooting at sight any and every Indian regardless of tribe or condition is a tradition and that it never be a historical verity.

Occasions like these are proper occasions for putting into careful historical form the records and original sources for the events which they commemorate. I have therefore made it part of my plan for this address today to give reference to all the original sources of the story of the Wiseman Massacre, and where they may be found. There were not many frontier newspapers in Nebraska, Dakota, and Western Iowa in 1863. The files of many of these for the months of July, August, and September of that year, no longer exist. In the state Historical Society newspaper collection at Lincoln is only one original source on this subject. It is found in the Brownville Advertiser of August 22, 1863, and reads as follows:

From Sioux City IA. Aug. 7, 1863
Editor Advertiser: "It seems to me that the whole northwest is destined to be forever revolutionizing: The Indians are never long at peace with each other, ignorant and degraded as many of them are, they are not capable of ruling, nor yet of being ruled; but I, dwelling among them as I now am, am forced to feel in some degree the deplorable effect of the Indian wars which threaten to deluge the whole of this beautiful country and lovely land in blood."

"We are called upon to record one of the most fiendish, atrocious acts ever perpetrated on the northern frontier, in which three children were brutally murdered in cold blood, and two horribly mangled. The oldest was a girl of about sixteen years, which had been left by her mother to take care of the family while she went to Yankton, a short distance from where she resided. As she returned, on approaching her residence, she saw an Indian hastily disappearing behind the house. She hastened back to a small village before entering the house, and immediately returned with six men, who gained admission to the premises only to discover to the stricken mother the mutilated corpses of her children, and two others which had probably been left for dead."

In the Omaha Public Library is one additional original reference. It is found in the Omaha Nebraskian of August 7, 1863, and reads as follows:

"We learn from a letter received by the wife of Captain Tripp, of Company B, Dakota Cavalry, who is now on a visit in this city, that a party of four Indians visited the residence of Mr. Wiseman, four miles south of St. James, N. T., on or about the 25th inst., and, in the absence of the parents, killed five children, the eldest a girl of sixteen and the youngest a boy of six years of ages. They also stole several valuable horses. A detachment of fifty soldiers has been sent in pursuit of the Indians, but there is little probability of their capturing them as the Indians had three days start."

In Sioux City there are no newspaper files or clippings containing original references to the subject. It is possible there are newspapers in the Historical collection at Pierre, South Dakota, or Des Moines, Iowa, and I have written there. If any are found they will be incorporated in this record.

In the report of the commissioner of Indian Affairs for 1864, on page 284, is the following references in the annual report of W. A. Burleigh, U.S. Indian Agent at the Yankton Indian Agency, dated Greenwood, Dakota Territory, October 21, 1864.

"When General Sully got ready to move up the Missouri, in June last, with his expedition, he took into the service of the United States, or rather directed me to do so, fifty reliable Yanktons to act as scouts, and left them under my charge. As a compensation for their services, they received arms, ammunition, clothing and rations. As the expedition moved up the Missouri river, it was feared that small war parties might travel down the James or Dakota river, and rob and murder our citizens. I directed these scouts to divide into two parties. One detachment was sent up the James about two hundred miles to destroy a famous rendezvous of these hostile bands, known as the Dirt Lodges, while the other was sent to protect the country between the Missouri and Sioux Falls. The force sent against the Dirt Lodges proceeded to that point and utterly destroyed the village, drove the hostile bands more than a hundred miles beyond, punished them severely, and returned. The party patrolling the country between the Missouri and Sioux Falls overtook a war party on their way down the Vermillion, arrested the ringleaders and shot them on the spot. Before their execution two of them confessed to having killed two white persons in the Minnesota massacre, and five children in one family in Nebraska the last year. (This was the family of Mr. Wiseman.)"

In the Centennial history of Cedar county written by Lewis E. Jones and read July 4, 1876, at the celebration in St. Helena, on page three of the printed pamphlet is the following brief reference. "Another drawback on Cedar county, as well as the surrounding counties, was the dread of hostile Indians. Immediately following the dreadful massacre at Mankato, Minnesota, a whole family of five children, those of Mr. Wiseman, near the settlement of St. James, were most brutally slaughtered by these inhuman fiends. This occurred in 1863. Dr. Lorenzo Bentz was also killed the following spring, in 1864, a few miles northwest of St. Helena.

"Whilst the children of Mr. Wiseman were killed, he himself, together with several citizens of this county, had volunteered in a military company as Home Guards, expecting to defend their own firesides, but were ordered to join Sully's expedition against the Indians. Thus our thinly settled frontier was deprived of several of our best men during those troublesome times."

This is important because the writer was himself a settler in Cedar county in 1858 and a continuous resident during the period from that time for the next forty years.

But by far the most original source of historical information on the Wiseman Massacre is contained in this little pamphlet which I hold in my hand. It bears a title as follows: "A Brief History of the Massacre of the Wiseman Children." It was written by Henson Wiseman himself in 1894 and printed in that year. It is a printed appeal by him for justice from the United States government and payment by Congress for the loss he sustained in the service of the United States army by the murder of his children and theft of property. It is one of the most pathetic documents in all Nebraska history. It tells the story of his enlistment; his parting from his family; the news conveyed by shoes found in Indian hands; his home and his meeting with his wife. It then tells in a few words the story of his subsequent life and appeal to Congress to pay for the property stolen and the children murdered. It is written in a simple, direct way, as a frontiersman would write. It closes with this appeal:

"Now to a candid world. If I should treat one of my neighbors as I have been treated by the government, I would have been put out of sight long ago. Thirty-two years have passed. I did not live on government land nor on the Indian's hunting ground. But forced in old age to hard labor; my life made miserable; my family buried in blood, dirt and rags, like so many dogs; their mother not able to see them to their resting place. I received an honorable discharge from the army, but not from dread of duty. Those Indians stole from me for four years after all this. I was on my guard and was shot at."

"I wore a Colt's revolver for five years, night and day, and during the day I spent the time working for my bread, and at night examining the country for miles around to be sure that no Indians would be in waiting at dawn of day, as I knew their intentions were to kill me. I employed a young man for one year to act as scout for me, at $25.00 per month."

"I now make one more appeal to congress that my claim may be settled according to the invoice filed in congress years ago. (See invoice record of Dakota county, Nebraska.) I now appeal to law and justice. Paddock and Saunders having failed, and senator Hitchcock having died while the matter was pending in congress. Will the representatives and senators from Nebraska, as well as all members of congress, do for their humble servant what is just? I, an American citizen 77 years old, beg an-immediate-settlement."

These are all the original sources as yet discovered by me in my search. It is my purpose to pursue the search and to put into this record everything of an original nature which may be found. We shall then have available for the future historian and literary writer the story of this tragic event so far as it may be known from the original sources.

What Indians murdered the Wiseman children? In his appeal pamphlet Henson Wiseman says the deed was done by the Yankton and Santee Sioux. Probably, he should know better than any other man. But no proof is offered by him and survivors saw and described the Indians. The Yankton Sioux tribe were the nearest Indians to the Wiseman home. For two hundred years and more the tribe had lived on the North bank of the Missouri at that point. But the tribe, as a tribe, was never at war with the White people. In fact, the chief of this tribe notified white settlers in the summer of 1862 of the impending massacre and thereby the lives of many white people were saved. The Santee tribe of Sioux did not live in Nebraska then. Their homes were on the border of Minnesota, more than 200 miles from the massacre. But they had been driven from their homes and scattered by the military, following the great Minnesota massacre.

The most direct evidence we have is in the report of Indian Agent Burleigh who says that his Yankton Sioux scouts shot two Indians who confessed to taking part in the murder of the Wiseman children. But he does not say to what tribe or band these Indians belonged.

We are met here to commemorate the most outstanding event in Northeast Nebraska in the conflict between the White race and the Red for the possession of this beautiful region. It is altogether fitting that we should do this.

No event of which I know has so much dramatic and human interest in the settlement of this section as the Wiseman tragedy. It is full of appeal. It is full of sacrifice. It is full of characteristic frontier incident.

The women of this community have done their part well. They have not waited for a state appropriation. They have not waited for the United States Government, even, to recognize the result of its own inadequate protection to these children and return to Henson Wiseman what they would not return to him when living, some satisfaction for the irreparable loss which came to him while in the service of the United States. These women of Wynot and Cedar county have done wisely not to wait. They have recognized the privilege and duty of raising a fit memorial to the memory of this family. And they have done it while there are yet living representatives of the Wiseman family and neighbors who knew the family in pioneer days. These women have rightly judged that in this rich land of northeast Nebraska, in Cedar county, and in Bow river Valley, there is plenty of wealth to spare in the possession of those who have inherited without price the great opportunity of making wealth on Nebraska soil purchased by the lives of these children and by the lives of thousands of other brave pioneers along the border. So I greet the women of the community who have made this memorial possible and in their name and the name of the Nebraska State Historical Society, I salute the people of the hundred other communities in Nebraska where a similar work is called for the historic memories of the place.

What does the memorial signify? What story does it tell a hundred or thousand years hence to the people who live in this valley and to the tourists who shall come to visit this shrine?

The frontier home. No other home in any time of place like the frontier home. Why? Because the frontier home was built and is built by the hand of the men and women who live in it. Nothing endears home so much as the labor of the hands and the brain which goes directly into the walls. I have cut the logs and raised them. I have cut the sod and piled it in the wall. I know whereof I testify. No matter how rude. The frontier home stands above every other home of these later years in its significance to the human soul. So this memorial signifies the frontier home.

Childhood. This memorial forever speaks of childhood. The childhood of a new land. The children of a simple trust, fearing no danger, confident and loyal to the home. Thousands of children have stayed at home alone before and since the Wiseman children stayed here. Only the rare few of these thousands have met such fate as the Wiseman children met. Out of the pioneer children of northeast Nebraska the Wiseman children were chosen by fate as typical heroes and heroines of the frontier time. And this memorial of granite forever witness to their name and their devotion.

A man's devotion to home and defiance of orders. Always think of the Wiseman frontier tragedy with Henson Wiseman as the central figure. He typifies the supreme thing in frontier life and in the life of this nation. I see him riding across the plains, foodless, absent without leave, regardless of proper military discipline, I see him standing at the Fort Randall Stockade. I see him defy the commander to arrest him as he turns his horse's head towards his log cabin home. I believe, as every good citizen believes, in law and order. I believe in military discipline and I have lived under it, but above and beyond all of these I believe in the supreme duty of a human being to protect his home and to respond to the wise summons of duty as it appears to him. And so I glory in the figure of Henson Wiseman defying military discipline and riding to the call of home. We shall always have in history of the world the great mass who takes orders and obey discipline, who live obediently under the rules and regulations which society has made. We have had at long intervals and shall have, I trust, men and women who break the rules, who disobey orders, who defy discipline for a great cause and to a great end. These men and women constitute the hero role of the human race. I cannot undertake to name them now. Some of them were the moving spirits in the American Revolution of 1776. Some of them are living in our own life time and we are not wise enough yet to know them.

So this memorial may always stand for the spirit of Henson Wiseman, the frontier soul, faithful enough to the institutions of his time to take the oath and wear the uniform and fearless enough for a supreme cause to defy discipline, to disobey orders and to ride across the wilderness in response to the supreme call of human duty.

This speech was duplicated from a family member's copy.

This is the Wiseman Monument which was erected to honor the massacred children of Henson and Pheobe Wiseman. It was unveiled Sunday June 6, 1926, by Laura Wiseman Lawson. John Wiseman, Henson's son who was away in the civil war at the time of the massacre, was to unveil the monument, but passed away one month before. In the top picture you see John Wiseman's house that was moved to the memorial site, and has since then, deteriorated. In 1976 the current cabin (bottom picture) was built by Leroy Beste, Don Deblauw, Don Hochstein and Larry Hochstein, for a local Centennial parade. It won many first place honors in surrounding parades that year, and then was placed on the memorial site. There is also a rock mound, that looks like a chimney, that encases a guest book for visitors.

This is the front and back side of the stone at the monument site. There are a few mistakes on it. Wiseman is misspelled Wisesman; Hannar could be Hannah and the 24th should be the 23rd. There are also discrepancies in the children's ages, if you compare them with what Henson has written in his letter and if you also compare them with the cemetery stone. If the cemetery stone is correct, their ages would have been 15, 14, 10, 8 and 4.

Dedicated to the Memory of Hannah Wiseman.

In 1863, Below St. James, in Cedar County, Nebraska, a Young Girl, Hannah Wiseman, Was Killed by Indians. To Her Memory These Lines Are Dedicated.

Peace reigned in the silent village
　　Of the Indian tribe,
In the bosom of the forest
　　By the river side;
Sleeping lie the savage Poncas
　　On their hairy bed,
While Aurora in the heavens
　　Paints the cloudlets red.
And a gentle Indian maiden
　　Restless slumbers now;
Her the Eagle of the nation
　　Did his love avow.
And a silent tear escapes
　　From her closed eye,
And her gentle bosom raises
　　With a mournful sigh,
For the warriors of the nation
　　Buried have the pipe,
And the paint of red and yellow
　　Now their faces stripe.
And the Eagle, bravest warrior,
　　Went to distant lands;
To the lakes the spirit haunted
　　With his Indian bands;
And she sees him in her slumbers;
　　Sees him in her dream;
Where the Elkhorn's blooming woodlands
　　Shade the silent stream.
' Round the council fire standing
　　Neath the morning star;
Gathering are the dusky warriors,
　　On the path of war.
Here midst all those mighty nations,
　　Stands the Eagle brave;
And the warriors he addressing
　　Them, this council gave;
"Warriors of the greatest nation
　　Of Missouri's slope;
Listen to the mighty Eagle,
　　Of the Antelope.
Where the meadow lark is singing;
　　And the wild dove coos;

In the land of Minnetonka;
　　Is the home of the Sioux.
Our homes are now invaded
　　From the emerald seas,
And the pale fac'd, blue-ey'd Yankee
　　Blazes our trees;
And the white men without rev'rence
　　Our spirits shock,
With the pickaxe desecrating
　　Our sacred rock.
Our tribes were never beaten;
　　Masters are we here;
And the land of our fathers
　　We from foes must clear.
Let the tribes in countless numbers
　　As the drops of rain,
Sweeping thro' the field of battle
　　Like the hurricane,
Kill the settlers without mercy,
　　Lay them in the dust;
Keep the fair-haired, blue-eyed maidens
　　For the warrior's lust;
Take the scalp, the battle trophy,
　　Take it without fear;
Let it tell to all the nations,
　　We are masters here.
Paint the war post red and yellow,
　　Make it strong and high,
Let the voice of all this nation,
　　Raise the battle cry."
And the dusky, painted, warriors
　　Silent stood about
Till the chieftain of the nation
　　Raised the battle shout.
Then they struck the painted war post,
　　Struck it yet again,
And each warrior sank his hatchet
　　In the wood's tough grain,
And they turned their faces northward
　　In true Indian style,
Followed they their leader's footsteps
　　Then in single file;

And they went forth through the morning,
    Through the heat of day,
Till the shadows of the even
    On the prairies lay.

II.

Where midst maple's silver branches
    Hidden owlets sleep,
And the bees with drowsy humming
    Their sweet harvest reap,
Where the pure and crystal waters
    Of the winding Bow,
Slowly through a fruitful valley,
    Ever onward flow.
Here midst wheatfield's golden harvest,
    In a pleasant nook,
Stood a settler's humble cabin
    Slept a maiden fair;
And her cheeks were like the roses;
    Dark brown was her hair;
With a smile upon her features
    In her peaceful sleep,
While the summer's gentle zephyrs
    Round her pillow sweep.
Ah, she dreams of pleasant meadows
    And the woodland's gloom,
Where the roses and the violets,
    And sweet flowers bloom;
Where, beneath the shady branches,
    By the rippling stream,
Was the heart within her bosom
    Waked by Love's sweet dream.
Here a young and handsome settler
    Asked her for his wife,
And to share his humble cabin,
    Cheer his lonely life.
She had blushingly consented;
    And she dreamed of times
When for her will ring the chorus
    Of the wedding chimes;
Of the time when from a distance
    Father word will send
That to his fair daughter's wedding
    He will give consent;
For her father has gone foreward
    Indians to subdue;
To protect the frontier settlers
    'Gainst the rising Sioux.

He has left his blooming children,
    Left them here alone
With the good and faithful mother
    In his prairie home,
And to stock the empty larder
    Mother has gone down,
Under Neighbor's kind protection,
    To a neighboring town.
Now within the silent cabin
    Sleeps the maiden fair,
By her side two little brothers
    In their sister's care;
Under heaven's kind protection
    Sleeping without fear,
While fair fortune hides her favor,
    And foul death draws near.
While the little stars are twinkling
    In the vaulted sky,
And the stream with pleasant murmuring
    Sings a lullaby,
Dusky warriors through the wheat field,
    In the shadows deep
That surround the settler's cabin,
    Stealthily now creep;
And within their savage bosoms
    Fearful thoughts are born,
While within, the hours measuring,
    Steady ticks the clock,
Till the children are awakened
    By the morning cock.
Slow the morning stars are fading
    In the early light,
And the shadows are receding,
    Of the peaceful night.
And the brother through the window
    In the early gloom,
Sees a skulking, painted Indian,
    Sees his waving plume,
And he rises from his pillow,
    Walks across the floor,
Grasps the ever-loaded rifle
    Standing by the door;
And he finds it very heavy
    For one of his years,
But he takes it to the window,
    Holds it without fears,
Aims it at the painted Indian;
    At the rifle's crack,
Moaning falls the hidden warrior,

In his savage track.
Then the echoes are awakened
    By a fearful yell,
To the frightened children sounding
    A last funeral knell,
Like the tiger in his fury
    Kills the silent doe,
So through the cabin go,
    And the girl is quickly butchered
By the furious ball,
    While her weeping little brothers
By the hatchet fall,
    And the Eagle, foremost warrior,
Swings the scalping knife red,
    With three strokes the scalp was taken
From the maidens head.
    Onward then the Indians hasten
Through the broken door;
    Leave the children lying
On the blood-stained floor,
    And the girl so heavy moaning
On her humble bed,
    Where she paints her snowy pillow
With her life-blood red.
    Morning passes and the sunbeams
Paint the world with light,
    Through the noonday's glaring sunshine
Until dewy night.
    Slow the blooming prairies darken,
Night again draws near,
    And the starry hosts of heaven
Slowly re-appear.
    Then a youth hastes thro' the val'y
Through the darkening grove,
    Where he seeks the sweetest flowers,
Picks them for his love;
    And he hastens through the shadows

Of the summer night
    Till he spies the gloomy cabin
In the starry night.
    As he nears, fearful forebodings
Through his bosom go,
    For the house seems awful silent,
Darksome, filled with woe,
    And he pauses in the clearing,
Calls his dear one's name,
    But from out the silent cabin
Nought but echoes came.
    He advances, slowly enters
Through the open door,
    And he sets his trembling footsteps
On the slippery floor,
    And stumbles o'er the bodies
Of the children slain.
    And he takes the unused candle
From the mantel frame
    And he lights it, then a horror
Tearful met his gaze,
    Where the children's swollen bodies
Lie in death's embrace,
    And his dear one so disfigured,
Horrible her head,
    Where she lays so pale and silent
On her bloody bed.
    Then he knows that by the Indians
Murdered was his bride,
    And he sinks down in his sorrow
Moaning by her side,
    And a fearful oath is taken
In his manly wrath;
    Woe, woe to the wretched Indian
Who shall cross his path.

Author Unknown

This was taken from the pamphlet that was handed out at the unveiling.

THE WISEMAN MEMORIAL
Erected by the Country Club of Wynot, Nebraska

By Mrs. J. G. Campbell, Pres.

On a summer's day sixty-three years ago on the 23rd day of July there occurred in this community one of the most fiendish deeds recorded in history.

In a wooded section where travel was almost unknown stood a small log cabin, the home of Hensen Wiseman, his wife and six children. They had no schools, no churches, no neighbors, mail but once a month and no comforts of life.

How will we be able to impress upon the minds of our children and their children the hardships and privations which our forefathers have endured? Only by keeping a vivid picture before them and their minds fresh with the events of early history, so they may be able to realize and partially visualize the hardships and struggles of the Nebraska pioneers and their noble loyalty and sacrifices in their defense of their country against the early Indian outbreak's.

In the fall of 1862 Hensen Wiseman enlisted in Company I, Second Nebraska Cavalry, for scout service against the Indians. He obtained a furlough about the first of June and came home to the log cabin to bid goodbuy to his wife and children. They clung to him, saying: "The Indians will kill us if you leave," and he answered, more like a soldier than a father: "No, the government will protect you."

So he left his wife and children to the mercy of the Indians. He was ordered into Dakota territory with General Sully and was stationed at Crow Creek, 200 miles away. On the 22nd day of July, Mrs. Wiseman took the stage to Yankton for necessary supplies and was gone over night. Returning the next day, she left the stage at St. James and walked to the home, a distance of about four miles.

Arriving home about dark and opening the door, she saw an Indian lying on the floor and the house in great disorder. Rushing around the house, she found a young boy on the ground dead. Concluding that all were dead, she fled to St. James, going through the brush so as to escape observation in case the Indians were still around. Arriving there, the citizens were too frightened to go back at once to the rescue. They waited until daylight and then an armed party on horses went to the cabin by the road. When they reached the cabin, they found the Indian was gone and three of the childred dead. One boy, aged five, lived three days and the only girl survived five days.

To commemorate the spot where the Wiseman massacre occurred and also mark the place of the first white settler in Cedar County, the Country Club of Wynot has erected this memorial to future generations of Nebraska. It is only fitting we should do this. The event is full of human interest, full of appeal and sacrifice and characteristic incidents. The Wiseman memorial was erected not to mark the spot of the bloody deed in history, but to commemorate the spirit of our forefathers in subduing that part of our former wilderness; to designate by a visible sign the beginning of an epoch of progress in civilization for us and for our posterity -- a sign to lighten our pathway to a higher plane of thought and living where our Heavenly Father wishes to direct our course.

What does this memorial signify? What story does it tell to the living of today? What story will it tell in a hundred or a thousand years hence to the peoples who live in the valley and to the tourists who will come to visit it?

In the memorial we have erected, the coming generations will have before them the true date of the massacre and the date of the first white settler in Cedar County. It will be a mecca for tourists from far and near, resulting in the determination of young people to live worthy of their early and sturdy ancestors.

The site chosen was the exact spot where the log cabin stood, a triangular piece of ground (the land being donated to us by Theodore Beste, a pioneer of Cedar County), and is one of the most beautiful spots in this part of Nebraska. When the club first talked of marking the spot a boulder was considered, but it was finally decided to erect a memorial that would be a credit to us as well as the community. Where the firplace of the log cabin was located stands this large, rugged slab. It is seven feet high, four feet wide and two feet deep and weighs 5,200 pounds. On the front side is the inscription relating to the massacre, date, names of the childred and their ages, and the date of settlement in Cedar County. On the reverse side are the names of the members of the Country Club.

The base of the slab is set in concrete, with a ten-foot square platform around the monument. It is enclosed in a beautiful four-foot iron fence, set in cement. An iron fence across the front makes the site very attractive. Inside the ground is a pilaster of stones (which were picked up by the club members) in which is an iron archive where a registry of visitors is kept, 730 having registered since the first of August. It may be an interesting item for the readers that all the material the fireplace was made of was broken up and used to fill in at the base of the slab. An old mule shoe found in the fireplace was placed in the cement walk leading to the monument.

The monument was dedicated June 6th, 1926, with impressive ceremony. Dr. A. E. Sheldon, of the State Historical Society, gave the principal address. Four five-minute speakers, a double quartet and two bands furnished other parts of the impressive ceremony. The unveiling of the monument was by Mrs. Laura G. Lawson, only living child of Hensen Wiseman. Over 2,000 people were in attendance. It was on this day the Country Club felt repaid for all their efforts.

Just a few words telling how we raised the money to accomplish our work. It was by work--hard work. Our club, composed of twenty farm women, was organized nearly seven years ago. We met twice a month to become better acquainted and for a social afternoon. Then our attention was called to the fact that we might be doing something to help those less fortunate than ourselves. Since then we have spent very few idle meetings. A year and a half ago we undertook the means to raise funds for the erection of the Wiseman memorial, still keeping up our charitable work.

Our first supper, netting us $100, gave us encouragement to go on. We gave a chicken supper, a bazaar, apron sales, bake and pastry sales, held a picnic supper at the monument grounds, did sewing, pieced and made quilts and sold them, tied comforters, made dozens of tea towels to sell--all this meaning a great deal of work; but we were recompensed for our efforts, the public enter-

ing into the spirit of our work and responding very generously. The club
members solicited the towns of the county and all responded very liberally.
Clubs, societies, schools of Cedar County, the State Historical Society.
Sons of the Revolution--all remembered us with donations. The ground,
the iron fence across the front and much of the labor, and all the printing
and advertising being donated, has helped us a great deal. It was a big
undertaking, but the best part of it is we do not owe a dollar. We are busy
at present working for our bazaar and supper to be held soon to raise funds
which we will use in beautifying the grounds, landscaping, planting shrub-
bery and flowers, and hope to make it one of the beauty spots of Nebraska.

It is the aim and hope of the Country Club to sponsor the movement for
a State Park in connection with the memorial site and we are working for that
project. The site is ideal (the monument will be included)--natural timber,
beautiful ravines, with the land still retaining the virginity of the prairies and
timbers of northeastern Nebraska, would in this way preserve the land from
which the present fields would have been builded.

I sincerely hope that this achievement of ours will be an incentive to
other rural clubs of Nebraska to commemorate some historical spot in their
own community or erect a memorial to some worthy citizen.

--Mrs. J. G. Campbell,
Pres. of the Country Club.

MEMORIAL SERVICE HELD AT MONUMENT

A Good Program and Ideal Day Make for Success of Annual Event

The annual roll call and memorial program given by the Country club at the Wiseman monument last Sunday afternoon was the most successful event of this nature yet held. A perfect summer day and the beautiful settings at this notable spot all helped to crown this event as the success that the ladies had carefully planned Besides the local people, visitors came from many other points Dixon county—Maskell, Newcastle and Ponca—had large delegations; Hartington and other points of the county were well representd and there were also many here from Yankton Vermillion and other South Dakota points.

The program was one of the best ever given at this annual gathering, the ladies of the club having carefully and successfully arranged the numbers. Congressman Edgar Howard, who had expected to be present and make the main address, was unable to come on account of serious throat trouble that prevented him from speaking.

The program was opened by Rev. Meyer, Baptist minister of Obert and the Hartington band gave several selections that were much appreciated. A male quartet from Maskell gave some very good vocal selections and Mrs. C. B. Butler and Rev. Meyer sang a duet that was very fine. Neva Thorpe and Miriam Sulivan also sang a duet. Paul Morris of Hartington gave some old time violin selections that were enjoyed.

Mrs. J. G. Campbell of Vermillion, former president of the club and the prime mover in building the Wiseman monument, was present and had charge of the program. She also gave the address of welcome and a short

history of the club and the monument. Former congressman J. J. McCarthy of Ponca was present at the gathering and gave a short and very humorous address, also paying high tribute to the pioneers of northeastern Nebraska and the ladies who had marked the spot of one of the most tragic events of the pioneer Indian times in this locality.

P. F. O'Gara, illustrious native Cedar county son and a leading attorney of Hartington, gave the principal address of the day, it being devoted largely to a touching tribute to the early settlers of the county, who blazed the way and underwent the hardships that were inevitable in settling a pioneer country.

A short talk was made by the veteran L. P. Lauritzen of Hartington, one who had known intimately and been a neighbor of the Wiseman family, and Geo. Hans, sr., also made a short talk.

ANNUAL PICNIC AT WISEMAN MEMORIAL

Varied Program Is Held and Large Crowd Is in Attendance. 1931

An ideal summer day greeted the Country club in their annual roll call and summer picnic held at Wiseman memorial park last Sunday. This remarkable beauty spot of northeastern Nebraska was the mecca of large crowds from many parts of the county, with a liberal attendance of the old settlers from the South Dakota side of the river. Many of the oldest life long settlers of the county were there to enjoy the social contact and talk over the early day times and experiences.

The program this year was much out of the ordinary, there being no regular addresses. Mrs. J. G. Campbell, leader in the organization of the Country club and one of the prime movers in erecting the Wiseman memorial, was over from Vermillion, accompanied by Mr. Campbell and the family. She gave a short history of the club and the memorial. A few old settlers gave short talks in keeping with the occasion.

A program of sports and contests was greatly enjoyed, small prizes being given to winners of the various contests.

Mrs. C. Lawson, only surviving daughter of Henson Wiseman, as the oldest settler present, was given a badge of honor. Mrs. Lawson was born in Cedar county and has lived here practically all her life of 64 years.

Mr. and Mrs. Wm. Gowery, being the oldest resident couple present at the picnic, were given a beautiful boquet, and Mr. and Mrs. Frank Thoene and Mr. and Mrs. Henry Anderson were awarded second and third places of honor.

The following awards were made in races and contests:

Straight foot race—Constance Nelson of Sioux City.

Wheel barrow race—Leslie Brown and George Wuebben.

Handkerchief race—First to Faye Miller and her group of five girls.

Rabbit race—Louis Denny first.

Shoe race—Herman Koch first.

Pie eating contest—Leslie Brown first.

Fat man's race—Geo. Beste loser.

In the pillow case race there were six on each side and the winners were awarded "suckers."

Women's potato race—Mrs. George Morten first.

Banana eating contest—Geo. Wuebben first.

Pop drinking contest—Thos. W. Denny first.

Nail driving contest—Mrs. Earl Thompson first.

Husband calling contest—Mrs. C. B. Butler first.

Sandwiches, coffee, ice cream and cold drinks were served on the grounds and were liberally patronized by the visitors.

The members of the Country club and their families enjoyed a picnic dinner and supper on the grounds. A free will offering to assist in improving the log cabin and grounds amounting to $3.15 was received.

The whole affair was one of the most successful yet given by the club.

ANNUAL ROLL CALL IS MUCH ENJOYED

Country Club Holds Picnic and Greets Visitors at Monument Park. 1933

Last Sunday was annual roll call of the Country club and it also marked the seventieth anniversary of the massacre of the Wisemen family east of old St. James in Cedar county.

The ladies of the club and their husbands and members of the families met at the park early Sunday and the day was spent in picnicing and in greeting many visitors and friends. The day was one of the most ideal of the spring and attracted hundreds of visitors and sight seers to this beautiful spot.

The annual roll call was conducted by Mrs. J. G. Campbell, first president of the club and who had much to do with the successful undertaking of erecting the splendid monument in memory of the massacre. Mrs. Campbell gave an appropriate address following the roll call, but there was no formal program.

Among the visitors last Sunday were residents of many towns in this vicinity and from the South Dakota side.

ANNUAL ROLL CALL IS A HAPPY EVENT

Country Club Plans Observe Massacre Anniversary Next Year. 1932

The sixth annual roll call and picnic of the Country club was held Sunday at the Monument grounds. A picnic dinner at noon was enjoyed by all. The afternoon was spent in visiting and renewing old incidents of the early days.

Roll call of the members by the first president, Mrs. J. G. Campbell, was responded to by eleven members. Of the six charter members of the Country club left, five were present Sunday.

Next year will be the 70th anniversary of the massacre and the members are already planning on appropriate exercises for the day.

The cabin was especially attractive, decorated in the club colors, old rose and gray, with garden flowers on the table and fire place and the braided rugs on the floor made by the club members, gave the cabin a real homey appearance.

A daguereotype picture of Henson Wiseman and his son John placed on the fire place lends a note of historic interest.

Several visitors were present, T. Goodwin of Seattle, Wash.; an early resident of Cedar county and a personal friend of Mr. Wiseman, spent the afternoon with us and complimented the Country club in their work.

Mrs. Laura Lawson told several interesting stories of the life of her father.

After a late lunch in the afternoon the 75 who were present returned to their homes feeling as if another anniversary and roll call day had been profitably spent and all look forward to another year.

WISEMAN, ARTHUR

WISEMAN, ARTHUR deceased son of Henson Wiseman and Phoebe Ann Cross Wiseman, was born in Monroe county, Iowa, August 23, 1847 and moved to Cedar county, Nebraska with his family from Fort Des Moines, Iowa in July 1857. The Wisemans made a stay of a year in Sioux City, the father having gone ahead to prepare a place for the family. His only schooling was gratuitous private instruction from Mrs. Amos S. Parker and Elizabeth Saunders. When his father joined Sully's expedition he left Arthur (then fifteen years old) in charge of the family and the property. On the 23rd day of July 1863, he died a martyr of his trust, while defending the home against Indian marauders. The story of the Wiseman massacre which follows, has been gathered in the main from Henson Wiseman himself, Mary A. Marr, Elizabeth Saunders, John Aten, William C. Jones, Joseph Morton, and Mrs. Amos S. Parker.

In the year 1863 Henson Wiseman, his wife and five children were living in the northeastern portion of Cedar county, Nebraska. Their cabin consisted of two single-room log houses about 14x16, with an open hall between, all under one roof. This open hall had been closed up with boards. The north room was entered by a door on the east side and there was a door to the hall on either side. The south room had a window on the west side. The house stood on the west side of a ravine formed by the union of two others, just below the juncture.

Below the cabin a tributary entered the main ravine from the west. This ravine led to old St. James. The site of the old cabin is included in Theodore Beste's pasture, the east half of section 16, township 32, range 3 east. All that now remains are the ruins of a chalk-rock chimney, a pile of debris covered over with turf, and a locust tree. The place had been selected with admirable foresight.

Henson Wiseman discovered and captured a hive of bees, and began bee culture and became locally famous in that industry. The timber abounded in deer and wild turkey. From the Wiseman manse and woodyard

steamboats were supplied with fowl, honey, venison, catfish, garden truck and wood. The transportation by water brought them every coveted pleasure.

John Wiseman, the eldest son, was serving in the Federal army. Henson Wiseman enlisted in Company I, 2d Nebraska cavalry, which was ordered to join General Alfred Sully's command. Wiseman requested his wife to move to old St. James for greater safety, but she refused to leave her home.

Wiseman had not been on good terms with the Indians. They both feared and hated him. A few months before the massacre an Indian boy named Chaska (about three years older than Arthur Wiseman), belonging to the Yankton Sioux, told William Gyte that a family in the neighborhood would be killed about the time corn was in the roasting ear. Arthur Wiseman had whipped Chaska in a personal encounter.

On the 21st day of July 1863, Mrs. Wiseman left her home for Yankton, Dakota, to make some purchases, walking to old St. James. Russell Wilbur drove the stage between Ponca and Niobrara, and Mrs. Wiseman took passage with him to Elm Grove, opposite Yankton. Here she stopped over night with George A. Hall's family. When asked if she did not fear to leave her children on account of the Indians, she replied that there was not an Indian within 1,000 miles. The next morning she crossed to Yankton, made her purchases, and returned to Elm Grove, stopped the next night with Mrs. Amos S. Parker. The next morning, as Willie Parker started for school she remarked that her poor little children had no school. Mrs. Wiseman returned by the same conveyance which had brought her, and was delayed at St. James by a thunderstorm. Walking by the bottom trail, she stopped to talk with Mrs. Saunders, and just before reaching home sat down to rest, and was surprised that neither the children nor the dog came to meet her.

Approaching the dwelling she saw the yard strewn with books taken from the house, and going nearer she saw blood on her door-latch. Fleeing along the west side she stumbled over something in the grass. It was the dead body of little Henry, eight years old. Passing around the house, she looked into the window of the south room and saw Arthur and his eleven year old brother lying on the floor. There was every evidence that a terrible struggle for life had taken place. Going to the nearest door, she rushed in, but, thinking she saw a live Indian lying upon the hall floor, fled panic-stricken up the west ravine to old St. James. Nine men were there, but not one dared go to the scene of the massacre.

The next morning the terrible news reached the East Bow, when Henry Morton, Sr., Werner Marx, Henry Ferber, and Frank Stupbell went directly to the scene of the tragedy. The scene presented would freeze the blood. Henry lay in the yard, where his mother found him, shot in the back; Hannah, aged fourteen lay in the hall, shot in the mouth; Arthur and Andrew lay upon the floor of the south room. The stock of Arthur's gun was shattered and the barrel was bent, and he grasped his gun by the barrel with both hands. In the north room, Loren, aged four and one-half years, was sitting upon the bed dressed, with his arm about the post. He was stabbed in the right side, the knife entered the lung. He called for water and drank greedily, and when asked who had hurt him, replied "Indians." One squirrel gun was left and the guns used by the boys were not taken. An Indian will never take a gun with which an Indian has been killed.

Arthur, Andrew, and Henry were buried in one grave. Loren survived two days and Hannah a night longer. The bodies remained there till the spring of 1903 when, at the insistance of their sister Laura (Mrs. Christ Lawson), they were moved to the public cemetery of St. James and buried beside their mother and the brother, Richard.

No sadder tale than the Wiseman massacre was ever told; no braver hero than Arthur Wiseman ever yielded up his life to a battle against fearful odds. The brave Nebraska boy has had neither poet or historian to tell his story.

Sleep hero, in thy silent grave
Beside her form who bore thee.
Some card may open Fame's bright portal,
To tell the deeds to men unborn
And sing thy name immortal.

Henson Wiseman died in February 1912, at the age of Ninety-four.

This was duplicated from a family members copy, the original author is unknown.

The

Wiseman

Family

This is Henson Wiseman. He was born Nov. 5, 1817 in Harrison county, West Virginia. He was married to Pheobe Ann Cross at Parkersburg, West Virginia in 1838. He died Feb. 19, 1912 at the age of 94 years old. This studio portrait was taken in Norfolk, Nebraska in the 1880's. The Sharps rifle that he is holding is one he carried in nightly patrols. Another Wiseman rifle, an Eli Whitney percussion musket, is at the Museum of Nebraska History in Lincoln.

Here Henson is sitting in front of the log house that he built two years after the massacre. He built a total of three homes on his land. Also notice the two guns that he has. One is the patent 1850 Colt revolver that he carried with him day and night for five years in a row.

This is Pheobe Ann Cross Wiseman. She was born April 20, 1820 and died June 12, 1901 at the age of 81 years old.

This is Henson and Pheobe's oldest living son John. At the time of the massacre, John was away in the civil war, thus avoiding death. He was born Nov. 8 1843 and died May 2, 1926 at the age of 82 years old. This picture was taken March 11, 1916. He was married two times in his life, first to Lizzie, who died in May of 1872. They had two children, but both died. He later remarried to Francis Ann Vanover on June 26, 1878 or 79. They had no children.

This is Richard Wiseman, the child that Pheobe was pregnant with at the time of the massacre. He was born March 8, 1864, never married and died May 1, 1902 at the age of 38 years old. Here he is seen in his sled in Vermillion South Dakota. He was a cripple but still managed to sell fruit and honey to the local people. When he was out visiting, people would carry him to and from his sled or buggy.

This is Laura Wiseman and her new husband Nels Christian Lawson (from Denmark) on their wedding day. Laura was the last child to be born to the Wisemans. She was born Sept. 8 1867, married March 8, 1887 and died Oct. 10, 1932 at the age of 65 years old.

This is Laura and Nels's family. This picture was taken before 1923. Seated, left to right are: Nels Christian Lawson; Ella, Mrs. Oscar Bensen; Caroline, Mrs. Louis Radke; Laura Wiseman Lawson; and Effie, Mrs. George Bowder. Standing, left to right are: Bertha, Mrs. John Preisler; Pearl, Mrs. Willard Guy; Mary, Mrs. Claude Bledsoe. Many of these descendants children can still be found in northeast Nebraska.

History of Wiseman and Lawson Families

By: Ray Guy & Laura (Bensen) Bruce, 1992

Phoebe and Henson Wiseman's oldest son John was in the army fighting in the Civil War at the time of the massacre. After the war he came home and built a log cabin east of the Henson Wiseman place. There is no history on his first wife. His second wife Fanny (Noble) lived in the cabin. A Lee Noble lived with them. John died May 2, 1926. His cabin was moved to the Wiseman monument site.

Laura (Wiseman) and Nels Christian Lawson had six daughters. They were Bertha Mae, Caroline, Pearl, Ella, Effie and Mary Elizabeth.

Bertha (Lawson) married John Preisler in 1911. They lived in Obert, Nebraska. John died in 1918 and Bertha and her two sons moved to Wynot, Nebraska in the Joe Mather's house. Bertha moved in with her mother Laura (Wiseman) after her husband Nels died in 1923. After Laura's death Effie (Lawson) and her husband George Bowder bought the Lawson house and moved to Wynot, Nebraska. Bertha moved to the Bowder home in St. James. Later she moved back to Wynot and lived in at least two different houses. When she was no longer able to live by herself she lived for a time with her son "Pete" and his wife Audrey in Pasadena, California. Later she lived with her sisters Effie, Ella, and Pearl. After that she lived in nursing homes in Coleridge and Wausa, Nebraska until her death in 1985.

Caroline (Lawson) married Louis Radke in 1913. They lived south of Wynot. One day Caroline was climbing over the fence to shoot at some crows and accidentally shot herself and died in 1930. Their son Merton was 16 years old. In later years Louis Radke lived with Bertha (Lawson) Preisler in Wynot. Then he moved near Wenatchee, Washington to live with his son Merton and wife Amy until his death.

Pearl (Lawson) married Willard Guy in 1917. They lived on a farm west of Obert, Nebraska. In the spring of 1926 they bought the Wiseman homestead and lived there until 1953. At that time they moved to Hartington, Nebraska. Pearl and Willard moved back to the Wiseman homestead in 1955 and lived there until 1962. They retired from farming and moved to Wynot, Nebraska. In later years they lived in a nursing home.

Ella (Lawson) married Oscar Bensen in 1916. They lived on a farm two miles north of Maskell, Nebraska. The farm was one of several that were homesteaded by Bendick Bensen. His wife Sophie (Klopstad changed to Nelson) owned the farm. Ella and Oscar stayed on the farm until their son Emory came home from the Navy after World War II. Emory married Shirley (Blatchford) and they bought the farm from Sophie Bensen. Oscar and Ella moved to Maskell in 1946 and lived in the Neal Maskell house until 1948. They bought Mother (Sophie) Bensen's house up on the hill in Maskell. For additional Social Security benefits Oscar took a job in South Sioux City, Nebraska at the Agricultural Adjustment Association (AAA) office. Oscar and Ella lived in a trailer house in the back yard of their son Oren and his wife Daryle (Nielsen) at 409 West Ninth from February 1, 1956 to May 1, 1959. They moved back to Bensen house in Maskell. Oscar died in 1965. The Bensen House burned to the ground May 1, 1967. Ella lived with her son Emory (Mick) and his wife Shirley on the farm for two months. She then bought a house on the lower street in Maskell and lived there until her death January 13, 1972.

Effie (Lawson) married George Bowder in 1922. They first lived in the Strenzke place in St. James. Then they moved to the Charlie Ritter place northeast of St. James. Then back to St. James on the south side of the old highway 12 at the intersection going north of St. James. After Effie's mother Laura died George and Effie bought the Lawson house and moved to Wynot, Nebraska. Effie now lives at the Wakefield Nebraska Care Center. (Date, 1993) She Died December, 23 1994. Mary (Lawson) married Claude Bledsoe in 1939. They lived in Sioux City, Iowa where Mary was a registered nurse and Claude was a detective on the police force. They later lived with Pearl and Willard Guy on the Wiseman homestead then moved to Beresford, South Dakota. They lived there until their deaths in 1969 and 1970.

Here is a picture of Laura and John, at Laura's house, in Wynot. This picture was taken in 1923.

The massacred children of Henson and Pheobe Wiseman are buried in the Wynot City Cemetery, originally the St. James Cemetery, which is on the south edge of town. Their plot is located in the southeast part of the cemetery. Henson, Pheobe, John, Richard, Laura, Nels and all of the Lawson children, with the exception of Ella Bensen who is buried in the Maskell cemetery, are also buried there. John's grave is across the east-west driveway, north of the large Wiseman marker.

The front of the marker says:
    HENSON WISEMAN
    NOV. 5, 1817
    FEB. 19, 1912
    PHEOBE A.
    WIFE OF
    HENSON WISEMAN
    APR. 20, 1820
    JUNE 12, 1901

The back of the marker says:
    ARTHUR AUG. 23 1847
    HANNER JUNE 8 1849
    ANDREW JAN. 29 1853
    WILLIAM OCT 20 1854
    LOREN JAN. 19 1859
    THE ABOVE CHILDREN WAS
    MASSACRED BY THE INDIANS
    JULY 24, 1863
    RICHARD L
    MAR 8, 1864 - MAY 1, 1902
    CHILDREN OF
    H & P A WISEMAN

Articles

And

Stories

CDC 00174

REAL WEST

$1.00
NOVEMBER 1979

les of the American Frontier

For Ray Guy
p. 9
(Ky.)
B. Paul Chiccine
Page 9-9-16-11-51

HENSE WISEMAN'S REVENGE

DAVE RUDABAUGH, GUNMAN

JAIL

TACHEE-CHEROKEE WARHAWK

AUBRY'S RIDE FOR GLORY

NOREM

CHARLTON
PUBLICATIONS

HENSE WISEMAN'S REVENGE

by B. Paul Chicoine

Most of us wouldn't chase a driver who cut us off on the Interstate; it just isn't important enough to go after that nameless face. But in the Nebraska of 1863, something happened where one man thought it was very important to chase nameless faces...

Studio portrait of Henson Wiseman taken in Norfolk, Nebraska, in the 1880s. Sharps rifle he is holding is one he carried in nightly patrols. Another Wiseman rifle, an Eli Whitney percussion musket, is on display in Lincoln Museum.

THIS MEMORIAL IS ERECTED
TO THE MEMORY OF
THE CHILDREN OF
PHEOBE ANN AND HENSON
WISESMAN

ARTHUR, AGE 16 YEARS
HANNAR, " 14 "
ANDREW, " 9 "
WILLIAM, " 8 "
LOREN, " 4 "

MASSACRED BY YANKTON
AND SANTEE SIOUX INDIANS
JULY 24, 1863
BETWEEN 9 & 10 O'CLOCK A.M.

DATE OF SETTLEMENT IN CEDAR CO.
— 1857 —

Granite marker on old cabin site, 2 miles south of old St. James, was erected by Wynot Home Comfort Club in 1926. Name has been misspelled.

Until the massacre, Henson Wiseman might have gone down in Nebraska and western history as a simple yet obscure homesteader. Like thousands of other men who made their way west in the late 1830 s, or even like his neighbors who settled alongside him in the Missouri River bluff land in 1857, Henson might have spent his days on earth in simple sweat and toil, and be remembered by a frontiersman's tombstone and a line jotted in the Wiseman family bible.

But fate could not have been more cruel or more deceiving for the Nebraska sod-buster; in this case, cocking the hammer for a tragedy so ugly, so horrible, that one cannot stand on the peaceful knoll where it all happened without feeling the terror in one's bones.

Indeed, a father's revenge can spring eternal. Which is what his white neighbors and the red men believed — at least as long as 'Hense' Wiseman remained alive!

Henson Wiseman was typical of the young men who set off for the prairies of Iowa in 1839. Born in Harrison County, West Virginia (then part of Virginia), in 1817, Henson was recalled to be a serious young man, a "loner" long before he reached his twenty-second birthday. His parents were farmers in Virginia's Harrison County, but they also raised bees and carpentered to raise their meager hill-country income.

Young Henson was also a dead shot, a trait which would serve him well in his later years. With these skills and personality, it is left to speculation why the tall, dark Virginian remained a bachelor as long as he did. But in the spring of 1838 he married Phoebe Ann Cross of Parkersburg. With their first child soon on the way, the newlyweds settled down to farming in Harrison County.

Like most men of his age and time, Henson was an excellent husband and provider. Farming and carpentering kept the larder full; the bees Wiseman maintained produced a steady income.

But there was one vice Phoebe Wiseman had failed to detect in her strong young husband's eyes; Hense Wiseman had what locals referred to as an 'itchy foot.' So it was that Henson, Phoebe, and their newborn son John left their peaceful Virginia home early in 1838 and set off by covered wagon for new land in Iowa.

The Wisemans' journey took them to Burlington, Iowa. After crossing the Mississippi by ferryboat, there, they purchased a small farm and settled down. Henson found work in nearby Burlington, and three more children were born. After a few years they moved on to Fort Des Moines, where they again found land and carpentry work. But Henson was not satisfied. After 18 years and two farms, the wagon was once again packed and pointed for the sunset, this time for the Iowa border — and the Dakotas.

Sioux City, Iowa, was a boisterous river town of 600 souls in 1857 when the Wisemans' top-heavy farm wagon rolled down out of Correctionville at the junction of the Big Sioux, Missouri, and Floyd Rivers on Iowa's western border. Sioux City was a favorite jumping-off point for soldiers, squatters, and steamboat men embarking by river for the Rockies. The town marked the edge of civilization as well. Settlers venturing out along the Nebraska shore took their lives into their own hands in 1857. But this warning meant little to Henson and his clan.

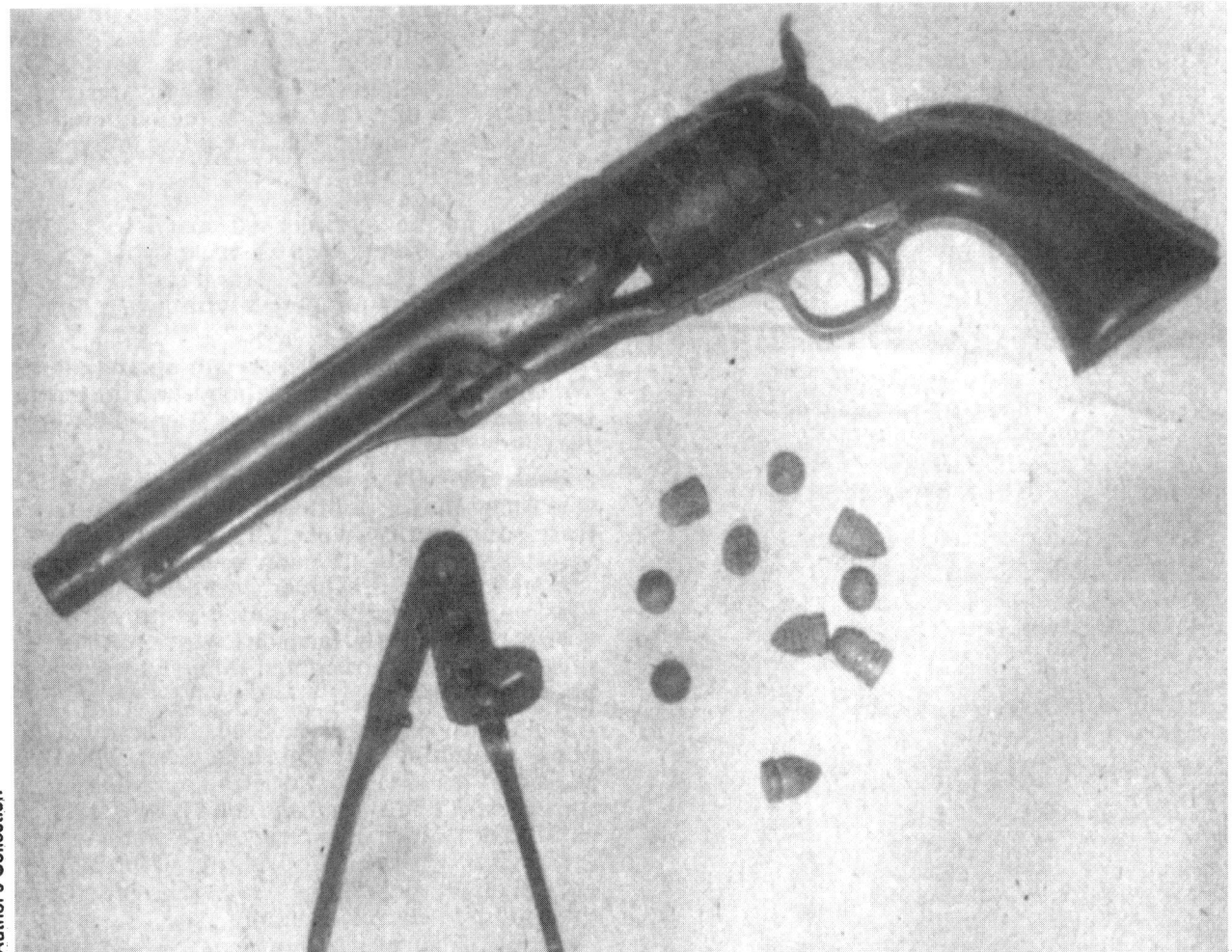

Author's Collection

Original Colt Army-version, cap-and-ball revolver (with mold and original bullets) owned by Vernon Guy, Wynot (Henson Wiseman's great-grandson). Wiseman worked and slept with this revolver for 5 years after massacre.

Wiseman and his family stopped just long enough to winter in Sioux City through 1857-58 before crossing the Missouri River to Dakota City, where they joined a wagon train heading west. This time six children clung to the swaying farm wagon as it joined the Niobrara caravan: John, 18; Arthur; daughter Hannar; Andrew; William Henry; and the baby Benjamin.

It was just over two weeks from departure that the wagon arrived in St. James, a small wood-landing village situated at the foot of the Missouri River bluffs and sixty miles west of Dakota City. Wiseman chose an isolated timber plot two miles back from the flatlands and the town. Being 18, John also filed a squatter's claim next to his father, and built his own small cabin.

A range of rugged hills flanked the St. James trail to the river, and it was between these ridges, at a point where two ravines meet, that Henson Wiseman built

a large double-log cabin. Over the years Henson had grown to distrust neighbors, in particular the red man. Thus the dog-run cabin he built commanded the rolling dooryard with heavy walnut logs and windows positioned for best defense.

Soon after their arrival, Hense discovered and captured a swarm of wild bees, which he relocated into homemade bee hives in the yard below the cabin. Wiseman's bees and the honey they produced added to the family's woodcutting income. The dense timber on both sides of the farm provided a rich bounty of fresh meat as well, which the family added to their produce of fresh vegetables. Since St. James was a major stopping point for steamboats, captains of the many upbound mountain boats counted on this Wiseman produce to fill their meager stores as they took on fuel at St. James landing. Thus the Wisemans, like most of the hardy homesteaders who chose

this Nebraska bluff country, were quite 'well suited' by the time war clouds gathered.

The death of Benjamin Wiseman, age 3, in 1859 was Cedar County's first recorded death. Later that year, Phoebe gave birth to another son, Loren. These births and deaths in the Wiseman household set the stage for what was to come.

From 1857 to 1862, settlement along the Bow Creek and Niobrara country went off with little incident. Some years before, the United States Government had guaranteed peace with the local Santee, Yankton, and Ponca tribes along the Missouri River in exchange for annuities. These were shipped to the Yankton and Crow Creek agencies by steamboat.

Until white settlement in 1857, the river bluffs had been a favored hunting grounds for the Sioux and Ponca. East of St. James a formation of smoking pyrite caused Indians to revere this line of bluffs as sacred holy grounds, and they had been reluctant to give it up. After settlement, local settlers bowed to tribal wishes and gave the Indians and their hunting parties open access over the many trails that crisscrossed the hills. It was an unsteady peace at best, but most agreed that it was a better option than war.

Henson Wiseman's arrival changed all that. At least in part. Henson himself was an avowed "Indian hater," and allowed no red man to cross his ridges. On a number of occasions peaceful war parties found a Wiseman warning in a well-deflected rifle slug. Indians were not welcome on Wiseman land.

As hard-core Indian haters like Hense Wiseman continued to stir up hard feelings in this and other outpost settlements, anger and acts of suspicion erupted into bloody war. In 1862 the knife was loosed across the Dakotas. Settlements and homesteads went up in smoke. As the plains became one great battleground, the terrified homesteaders of St. James and Cedar County found themselves on the edge of a bloody battle from which death could descend any moment.

Following the New Ulm, Minnesota, massacres of 1862 and a series of local Indian scares, 50 men from Cedar County enlisted in Company 1, 2nd Nebraska Cavalry, then being formed in Dakota City 60 miles away. Henson Wiseman was one of them. The original enlistment records for the unit describe the St. James beekeeper as follows: "Name, Henson Wiseman; Age, 44; Height, 6 ft.; Complexion, dark; Eyes, dark; Hair, black; Born, Virginia; Occupation, farmer; enlisted at Dakota City, Nebraska, by Captain John Taffee. Term of enlistment, nine months.

Like his fellow enlistees, Wiseman signed up in belief that Company 1 would be sent back to Cedar County to serve as a home-guard unit in case of attack. Since Henson's eldest son, John, had enlisted in the Union Army a year earlier, this left only himself, if assigned, and his 16-year-old second son, Arthur, to guard the isolated homestead.

Company 1 enjoined Captain Taffee to explain the situation to headquarters. Instead, the volunteers were shown a deaf ear. To

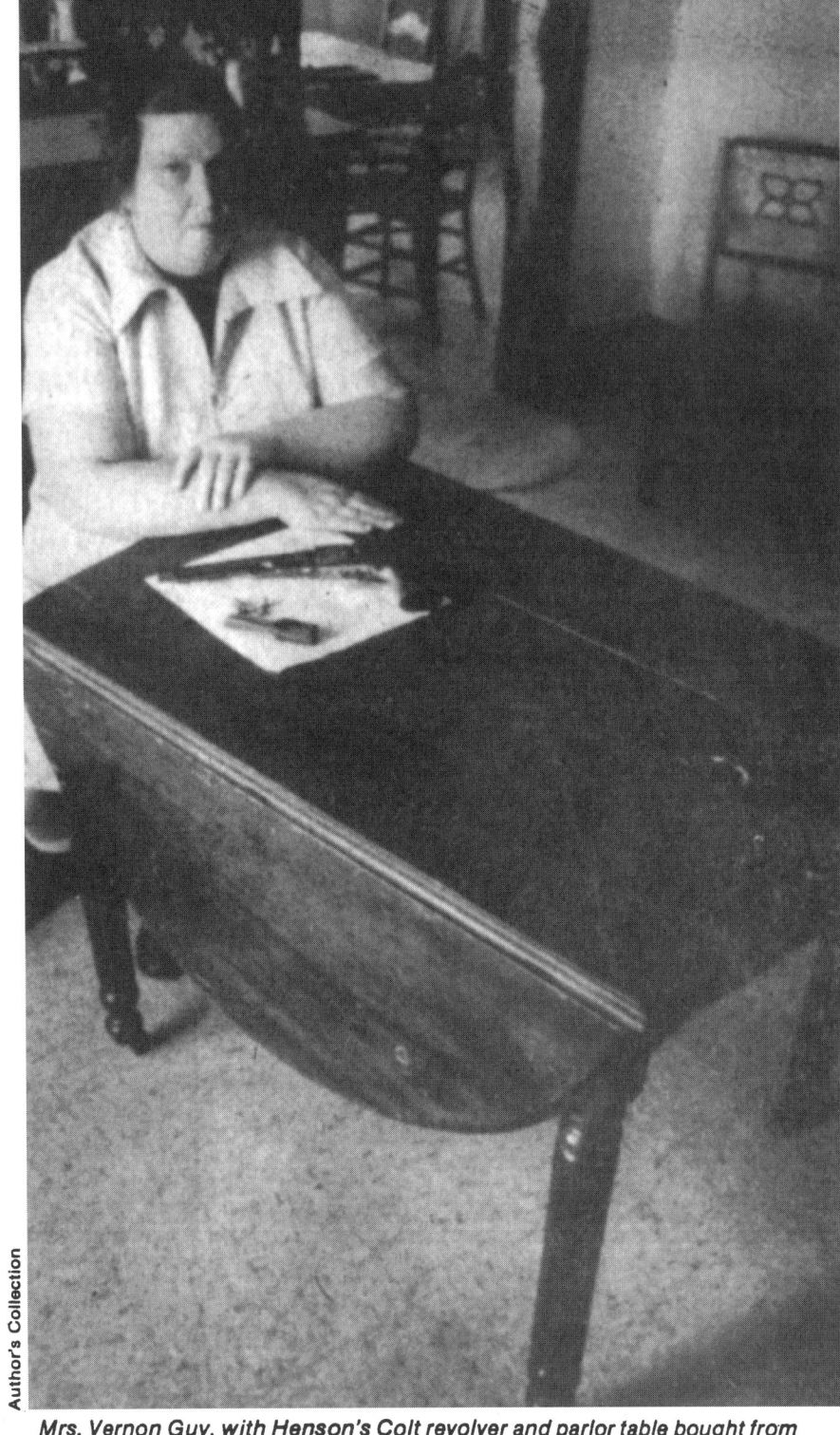

Mrs. Vernon Guy, with Henson's Colt revolver and parlor table bought from Virginia by Phoebe Wiseman, and in the cabin during Indian attack.

further complicate matters, Company 1 was restricted to headquarters in Dakota City until spring. Meanwhile, St. James remained unprotected through the winter of 1862-63.

In June 1863, General Alfred Sully took over military command in the Dakotas, replacing General Cook, who had failed to settle the uprising. Sully, an aggressive tactician and wise in

Indian warfare, ordered up the Nebraska and Iowa home-guard units, including Company 1.

Prior to departure, the volunteers returned to their farms for leave. By June, Phoebe Wiseman was expecting another child, but against her husband's advice she declined to leave the cabin for safe housing in St. James. The children did not agree with their

(continued on page 51)

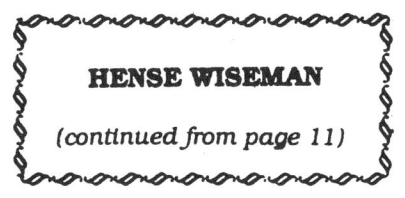

HENSE WISEMAN

(continued from page 11)

mother, begging their father "not to desert us."

With that the father left the isolated hill cabin. It was the last time he would ever see his children alive.

Soon after Henson's departure an incident took place on the Wiseman farm which offers a motive to later events. Arthur caught and severely beat a young Santee brave by the name of Chaska. Picking himself up off the trail where Arthur had throttled him, Chaska vowed retaliation. A few days later, William Gyte, a neighbor, overheard the Santee boast that "a family in the neighborhood will be dead by the time corn is in the roasting ear."

An alarm went out in St. James after the incident. Farmers and woodcutters from Yankton to Ponca gathered supplies in case of a siege. A delegation of settlers from St. James rode out to the Wiseman farm to warn Phoebe, but the Wisemans refused to leave.

On July 21, 1863, Phoebe Wiseman left her children, age 4 to 16, to guard the farm while she went to Yankton for supplies. Yankton itself lay some 20 miles west and across the Missouri River from Elm Grove.

Walking the two miles to St. James, Phoebe caught Russell Wilbur's mud wagon stage for the last leg of the 20-mile journey to Elm Grove. There she spent the night in the George Hall home before crossing by ferry to Yankton.

The next night at supper Hall asked the mother "if she didn't worry leaving her children alone for so long a time."

Phoebe, it is said, assured Hall and his wife that there wasn't an Indian within a thousand miles. She started for home the next morning.

Dawn broke warmly over the Wiseman cabin on July 23, 1863. Arthur, Andrew, and William Henry were working with the livestock when a volley of rifle shots exploded from the ravine below them. Caught by surprise and terrified by the line of

painted Santee rushing from the woods, the three boys scurried for the door. A load of buckshot caught 8-year-old William in the chest and killed him instantly. Arthur and Andrew made it inside. Within a few moments from their sudden assault, the attackers were in charge of the house.

A violent rainstorm delayed Phoebe Wiseman in Elm Grove the morning of July 23. Only with great difficulty did the Ponca-to-Niobrara stage reach St. James by late afternoon. By then it was almost dark. Muddy and near exhaustion, Phoebe climbed down from the dripping coach with her family's fresh supplies. A St. James neighbor begged her to spend the evening with them, but she graciously declined. So she came to the scene of Cedar County's worst family tragedy.

Approaching the yard along the twisting trail, Phoebe became apprehensive when the family dogs, usually alert to strangers, failed to run out to greet her. Pushing onward to the cabin itself, the mother found the darkened dooryard strewn with family books and papers. The front door bore a crimson bloodstain. The windows were splintered and smashed.

Desperation reached a crescendo as she fled along the cabin's west side. In the wet grass she found William's shattered body. Andrew and Arthur lay on the kitchen floor in a pool of dried blood.

Terrified, Phoebe ran back to St. James along the muddy path, now and then ducking into the dripping underbrush in horror of hostiles who might be following. When she arrived, soaked and hysterical, at the St. James store, men were roused and called to the general store.

The next morning, news of the massacre reached East Bow Creek. Henry Morten of East Bow assembled a posse, including Henry Ferber, Frank Stupbell, and Werner Marx, all farmers between East Bow and St. James. Crossing Bow Creek they circled into the hills south of the Wiseman timber and then down into the hollow. What they found, they described later, "was a sight to freeze the blood of anyone."

"They found three dead and two nearly so. The youngest boy *(Loren)* aged 5, could tell, 'the Indians scared me'. It was all he

ever said; he was stabbed under the left arm and lived three days. The girl *(Hannar)*, 15 years of age, as savages always do, bore savage infamy . She was alive and lived for five days, never speaking a word, but looking wildly around to anyone that came in her sight. The other three were dead; one boy, aged 8 years, was found outdoors shot through with a ball and three buck-shot. All the rest were in the house. The next boy *(Andrew)* ... was stabbed twice in the left side. The oldest ... *(Arthur)* ... had his head and arms all broken and mashed..."

The Wiseman children had put up a desperate fight in their last minutes. Arthur's rifle was shattered and bent. Another gun, empty, lay on the floor beside him. Since Phoebe had kept four loaded rifles in the cabin, the rescue party believed that two raiders had been killed, since the Santee never took a gun that had been used to kill an Indian.

News of the massacre did not reach Henson Wiseman until one month later. The post commander at Crow Creek impounded the letters from Wiseman's wife, in fear that the news would inspire his men to mutiny. Two Indians wearing white women's shoes appeared at the Crow Creek agency with news that "a white family had been killed near Yankton."

In a letter to the Nebraska Legislature thirty-two years later, Wiseman described a father's desperation in returning home to his family. In his later years Wiseman fought to gain reparations for property destroyed.

"...When the report reached me that it was my family, I was guarding some horses grazing two miles from camp. About daylight I mounted my horse and went to camp, knowing what was before me *(200 miles)*, I left without anything to eat, as I could get nothing until I reached Fort Randall, one hundred miles away. I traveled night and day until I reached home, stopping at the Fort two hours to get something to eat and rest my horse. There the commander of the post showed his authority. I showed fight and sixty rounds of cartridges, and told him that I was not a deserter but had been deserted..."

The father reached Yankton, South Dakota, the next day at

nine o'clock, where he reported to Captain Tripp's company, on the sick list. There he learned that Phoebe had been waiting for him in St. James, but had left for Sioux City, and in Wiseman's words, "was nearly insane."

He rode into St. James two days later, tired, muddy, and sick from his ride. Barely able to walk, he was shown the month-old grave of his children where they had been buried in the St. James cemetery. Arriving at the cabin, he found blood still dried upon the floor and the home still in shambles. A few days later, setting out after his wife, Wiseman found her wandering along Aoway Creek, over 20 miles east.

Twelve months passed before Phoebe was able to share with her husband the details of the massacre. The couple was without fresh clothing or shelter, as the cabin had been completely ransacked, and Phoebe could not be brought back to her home. On March 8, 1864, Phoebe bore a son "restless and under great trouble." The child would forever be retarded. For the Wisemans the tragedy had only started. Taking his remaining savings, Henson returned with his wife and newborn child to Virginia for a year. He returned in 1864, this time to rebuild, he later insisted, "what an uncaring government and the Indians joined to take from me."

Indeed, a change came over Henson Wiseman from that day forward, a change that bore the marks of a father's revenge and set them among the west's most tragic personalities.

If Hense Wiseman had been an Indian-hater before, now his fury knew no bounds. By his own admittance Wiseman became both 'hunter' and 'hunted.' For the next five years he led a double existence as farmer and hunter of Indians.

The details of Henson Wiseman's vigil are colored with the usual blend of fact and fiction pertaining to such matters. By his own account he "wore a Colt's revolver for five years, night and day, and during the day I spend working for my bread, and at night examining the country for miles around to be sure that no Indians would be waiting at dawn of day, as I knew their intentions were to kill me."

Never was Henson Wiseman far from his guns. With his army-issue Colt .44 at his side and his Sharps rifle in hand, he was a familiar sight stalking the ridges around St. James at night. For the most part, neighbors became accustomed to him. But Wiseman's insistence that he was being "shot at in the field" gave many of them reason for concern that Wiseman's vigil was being carried too far.

The mysterious death of Doctor John Bentz on a farm near St. James fueled that suspicion. Bentz, a bachelor physician and neighbor to the Wisemans, was discovered one morning slumped dead over his kitchen table, less than a year after the massacre. The isolated cabin had not been ransacked, and Bentz was known to have no known enemies except for Henson Wiseman.

Wiseman was brought in to St. James for questioning, but to no avail. Bentz had once been accused by the homesteader of "friendly intentions" toward Phoebe; but questioning by the sheriff failed to yield a strong motive. The investigation of Bentz's murder withered away.

John Wiseman returned from the army in 1865, and once again he and his father took up again where the war and tragedy left them. A new half-dugout cabin was built one mile closer to the river on John's timber tract, and the surviving family members moved in.

When Henson Wiseman was 77, he wrote the account of the St. James horror for the purpose of appealing to the U.S. Congress and the Nebraska Legislature — not for the deaths of his children, but for the substantial losses he incurred. Bitter and disillusioned by his personal loss as well as that of his wife, he wrote:

"Now, to begin anew, I had to pay taxes on property the Indians took. This was all done thirty-two years ago. I sent to the United States Congress a bill with affidavits of property, time and money lost, fifty dollars. Congress did not look at it. Ten years go by and I send in a petition signed by three governors, of two states and one territory. Senator Hitchcock was then in congress and he presented the bill which many citizens had signed, and congress refused to settle it.

"Now to a candid world. If I should treat one of my neighbors as I have been treated by the government, I would have been put out of sight long ago. Thirty-two years have passed. I did not live on government land nor on the Indians' hunting ground. But forced in old age to hard labor; my life made miserable; my family buried in blood, dirt and rags like so many dogs; their mother not able to see them to their resting place. I received an honorable discharge from the army but not from dread of duty. Those Indians stole from me for four years after all this. I was on my guard and was shot at."

Henson Wiseman never was to receive compensation for his losses. In 1912, at age 95, he died a broken-hearted old man and was buried in nearby Wynot along with his wife and son, Richard. In 1893, at the insistence of the Wiseman's youngest daughter Laura (born after the massacre), the bodies of the murdered children were moved from their mass grave in St. James to the Wynot city cemetery, where they now rest beside their father and mother.

The town of St. James was abandoned soon after the massacre. A new town by the same name was established one and one-half miles south of old St. James, near Bow Creek. One room of Henson Wiseman's second dug-out home is now part of the Vernon Guy farmhouse. In the house the Guy family carefully maintains two treasured relics of the St. James horror: a fine walnut parlor table which stood in the Wiseman cabin, and the Colt .44 Army revolver that the homesteader wore in his vigil.

In January of 1926, Henson's Eli Whitney rifle, which was left in the besieged cabin by Indians, was donated to the Nebraska State Historical Society in Lincoln, where it is maintained on display.

Today a large stone plaque near the Wiseman cabin site marks the spot where 5 children died that July morning in 1863. But those who knew Henson Wiseman or know of his vigil of revenge know that there's more to the story than just the names on this lonely stone.

War makes beasts of men, and victims of little children. **RW**

TRUE WEST

47305

LOST GOLD AT ROBBERS ROOST

April, 1975

NO FICTION

FRYING PAN CHARLIE

75¢

TRUE WEST
Frontier Times
OLD WEST
PUBLISHED IN THE WEST

UNDER THE DEVIL'S BLANKET

THE FATAL QUART OF STRAWBERRIES

GREAT FALLS' FIRST BLACK COWBOY

TICKET SCALPIN' ON THE RAILROAD

"RASCALS" and RANGERS

The Private War of Henson

The Wiseman monument. Note that the family name is misspelled and the date of the massacre is incorrect.

THIS MEMORIAL IS ERECTED TO THE MEMORY OF THE CHILDREN OF PHEOBE ANN AND HENSON WISESMAN

ARTHUR, AGE 16 YEARS
HANNAR, " 14 "
ANDREW, " 9 "
WILLIAM, " 8 "
LOREN, " 4 "

MASSACRED BY YANKTON AND SANTEE SIOUX INDIANS JULY 24, 1863 BETWEEN 9 & 10 O'CLOCK A.M.

DATE OF SETTLEMENT IN CEDAR CO. 1857

While fighting to protect others, Wiseman's own family was wiped out. He never forgot the perpetrators, and he never forgave the government for letting it happen

By SALLY McCLUSKEY

Photos Courtesy Author

IN 1863 the United States was embroiled in two wars, the Civil War and the war along the frontier in Indian Territory. Then Henson Wiseman defied the United States military and began his own war, along the woods and cliffs of the Missouri River in the land that bordered Pa Sapa, the Sioux holy grounds.

You can still go there, where Henson Wiseman lived and raged and fought his private war. The house is gone now, and the forest creeps closer around the little clearing every year, as if it would reclaim the scene where so much blood was spilled, where Pheobe Wiseman went mad with guilt and grief, and where Henson Wiseman waged his grim and lonely vendetta.

He and his wife, Pheobe, and their six children lived in a log cabin in Nebraska Territory, near the present town of Wynot. They had settled there when the Territory had been opened, under Squatter Law, for the land had not yet been surveyed. Wiseman built a two-room log cabin in a fertile stretch of land called the Brookie Bottom. He kept bees, and plowed with oxen, and cut wood for steamboats patrolling the Missouri.

At the outbreak of the Civil War his eldest son, John, enlisted. The family must have watched him set off with fear and misgivings in their hearts, yet fate was playing an ironic game with the Wisemans. John, far away in the midst of the conflict would live, unharmed; but the five remaining Wiseman children, aged four to sixteen, who remained at home, would meet bloody and terrible deaths.

All along the frontier the Indians were inflamed by broken or unfair treaties and the influx of whites. In 1862 the Santee Sioux rebelled in Minnesota, decimating the white settlers. Runners were sent to the southern Plains tribes, saying now was the moment to strike, for most of the soldiers had been called back east to fight other white men. War councils were called and along a 2,000-mile frontier, war parties began making forays. The whites, filled with fear at the stories they had heard of massacre in Minnesota, prepared to defend themselves.

16

Wiseman

Henson Wiseman was a fighter and no lover of the red man. Six feet tall, black-haired and dark-eyed, he was disliked by the Indians who lived and hunted near Brookie Bottom. When word went out that a home guard was being formed, Wiseman joined on as scout, enlisting in Company I of the Second Nebraska Cavalry in October 1862. Composed mostly of settlers, Company I was supposedly organized to defend white Nebraskans from the rampages of hostile Indians. Wiseman later said he enlisted because he felt the government "needed all the help it could get" to protect "the lives and property" of the settlers. He took his oath, put on his uniform, and obtained

a furlough to go home and say goodbye to his family, for his regiment was ordered to go into Dakota Territory and assist General Alfred Sully against the Sioux.

The Wiseman children were frightened at this news, and the younger ones burst into tears. They clung to their father and begged him not to leave, saying that if he left, the Indians would get them. But Wiseman was firm. Although he had hoped the home guard would stay and protect the Brookie Bottom area, he was sure that another regiment would come to guard the settlers. And with this assurance to his family, Henson Wiseman said goodbye, and rode off to protect the lives and property of Nebraska settlers in more immediate danger.

Pheobe Wiseman took her husband's word that she and the children would be safe, but no other soldiers came to Cedar County, where the Wiseman cabin was, and while Wiseman fought far to the north with the Second Nebraska Cavalry and the Sixth Iowa troops, his five children would be murdered.

IN July 1863, on the 21st, Pheobe Wiseman set off on foot to get supplies in Yankton, South Dakota, some fifteen miles away. The family was running short of provisions, and Indian troubles seemed like a distant dream. She left her eldest son, Arthur, in charge of the homestead.

Arthur was sixteen; he had a gun and his father's truculent spirit. A few months before, he had fought and whipped a Yankton Sioux youth named Chaska. Chaska had told a white man,

(Continued on page 44)

Henson Wiseman in later years, posing outside his cabin with his Colt revolver and shotgun.

William Gyte, that a family in the neighborhood would be killed "about the time the corn was in the roasting ear."

Apparently, the absence of any hostile action had caused Pheobe to regard Chaska's words as merely an idle threat. When a neighbor spied her and asked if she didn't fear leaving her children alone, Pheobe replied that there wasn't an Indian "within 1,000 miles." She crossed to Yankton, made her purchases, and began her return. When a heavy thunderstorm slowed her progress, she stopped in at a neighbor's. She was invited to stay the night, but refused for she wanted to get back to the children as soon as possible. Pheobe walked on, along a bottom trail, and stopped to rest so close to home that she wondered why the children and dogs hadn't heard and come out to greet her.

Picking up her parcels, she began the end of her journey, and at last reached the clearing. It was quiet. Something was wrong. Books were strewn across the rain-sodden yard, their limp pages stirring feebly in the wind. There was a wide smear of red across the door latch. Terrified, Pheobe broke into a run toward the cabin and stumbled over something in the wet grass. It was the body of her eight-year-old, Henry, shot in the back. She staggered to the door and saw Arthur and his ten-year-old brother, Andrew, lying on the blood-soaked floor. An Indian lay not far from them.

Certain that all five of her children had been murdered, Pheobe fled through the dusk. She was afraid to take the road, for fear Indians would find her, so she stumbled through the brush until she reached the tiny settlement of St. James, three miles away.

St. James had nine men, but none of them dared to return so soon to the scene of the massacre. The next morning the men rode out, taking a nine-mile route through the open prairie so no adversaries could ambush them. They came to the Wiseman cabin and found the five children. The dead Indian was gone. Henry's body lay outside the house. Arthur, his gun still in his hands, lay dead, his skull, arms, and hands crushed, the rifle barrel bent backwards. Andrew was dead beside him, shot. Hannar, the only daughter, fourteen, was not dead but was dying. The Indians had raped her, mutilated her with arrows, then put a cartridge in her mouth and lit it, tearing out her teeth. Hannar briefly recovered consciousness, but could only stare wildly about her, her eyes filled with terror. She died five days later. The youngest son, Loren, aged four, was found still alive, sitting up on the bed, his arm around the post. He asked for water, but the only other words he would say were, "Indians scared me." He had been stabbed in the left lung and died three days later. Arthur, Andrew, and Henry were buried in one grave beside the cabin. Loren and Hannar were buried beside them.

Pheobe, unable even to speak of what happened, was taken in and sheltered by neighbors. But after Hannar's burial, she slipped away from her protectors and ran away through the timber along the river. She could not be found.

IN the meantime, Henson Wiseman was in Crow Creek, nearly two hundred miles away, secure in his belief the he was helping keep the frontier safe for his own family and others. It was almost a month before he got word of what had happened to his children and his wife. He later maintained that neighbors had sent him letters, but that the army had seized them, fearing that if the Nebraska company heard of the Wiseman family's fate it would mutiny and return home.

Wiseman found out about the tragedy in a particularly cruel way. Some Indians came to the Crow Creek Agency, bringing with them spoils they said had been taken by some other Indians in a massacre in Nebraska Territory. Among the plunder was a pair of girl's shoes. They looked to Wiseman like Hannar's shoes, even to the patch he had put on them. Suddenly he was somehow certain that the family who had been massacred was his, and the murdered girl to whom the shoes belonged was his daughter.

Wiseman didn't ask for leave; he informed no one of his plans. With horrified suspicion in his heart, he took his gun, mounted his horse, and started the long ride home.

He later recounted his journey. "I mounted my horse and went to camp, knowing what was before me (200 miles). I left without anything to eat, and I could get nothing until I reached Fort Randall, one hundred miles away. I traveled night and day until I reached home, stopping at the Fort two hours to get something to eat and rest my horse; there the commander of the post showed his authority. I showed fight and sixty rounds of cartridges, and told him that I was the commander of that Fort and would shoot him on the spot; that I was not a deserter but had been

deserted. In twenty minutes Company 'A' of my own regiment, stationed there, came to me and told me to stay at the Fort as long as I wished, and leave when I was ready.

"They gave me all I wanted. I went to Yankton reserve that night and learned from an Indian interpreter all I wanted. I wrote a letter to my colonel 'to keep all the boys and fight the Indians when found, that they had gone up James River with what they had taken from me, and I would take care of myself and northeastern Nebraska'."

Wiseman reached Yankton the next day. At Yankton Reserve he had learned of the death of his children. At Yankton itself, he was told of his wife's derangement and disappearance. He finally reached the settlement of St. James, trembling with hunger and fatigue. At his cabin he saw the graves of his children and "blood all over the house floor, dried down twenty-five days." No one knew where Pheobe was.

Wiseman rested for several days in St. James, and those who knew the man said a terrible change had come over him. Finally he set out to find Pheobe. He headed for Sioux City, and met her on Aoway Creek coming back home. She could not remember where she had been.

Wiseman wrote: "She wailed and cried and tried to tell her grief but could not, and it was a year before she could tell it all. We returned to St. James the same day, and began at once to prepare some place to live. We had no home, nothing to live on, no clothing except what we had on our backs, which we had worn for many weeks. I knew we were in a hard climate and a hard place. Many is the time my poor wife would moan in her sleep and call for her children. I would then awake her, and she would moan and bewail the sad fate of her children and would finally sob herself to sleep."

Pheobe had been two months pregnant at the time of the massacre. On March 8, 1864 she had a baby boy. Wiseman wrote that the child was "born restless under great trouble, and for two years he would cry himself to sleep and wake up crying, and now, although thirty-two years have passed, is hard to reconcile in many ways and is entirely helpless." This mysterious, troubled, helpless son died shortly after Wiseman wrote of him. His parents apparently believed him to have been damaged by what Pheobe went through in those troubled months.

Wiseman was finally forced to take Pheobe and the child back to their native West Virginia for a year so she could recover her health and balance. He went $600 into debt to do so. Finally he, Pheobe, and their son returned to the clearing on Brookie Bottom. She regained her health and had another child, a daughter. But while Pheobe had broken under grief and finally recovered, Henson Wiseman had given himself to hate and was starting to become a legend.

IN CEDAR COUNTY it is still maintained that Henson Wiseman changed forever on the day he rode up to his cabin and saw his children's blood staining the floors. He swore vengeance upon the whole Indian race. Ever after, he carried

rifle with him, and he carried a Colt
pistol—in his own words, "five years,
night and day." He wrote that "during
the day I spent the time working for my
bread, and at night examining the country for miles around to be sure that no
Indian would be in waiting at dawn of
day, as I knew their intentions were to
kill me. I employed a young man for
the year to act as scout for me, at $25
per month."

Wiseman, it was said, always carried
his rifle with him, "ready at the sight
of an Indian to level the loaded rifle and
fire." An old Nebraska history book gives
this chilling description of him—that
after he learned of his children's deaths,
he was crazed by the event and "shot
Indians on sight thereafter, always leaving their bodies in attitudes of prayer."
Two extant photographs show him as an
old man, craggy of face, gun in hand, but
how many Indians he killed is not at all
certain. Two witnesses told of seeing
Wiseman pick off Indians as they canoed
down the Missouri. One of the witnesses
was a victim himself, an Indian Wiseman
had wounded. The other was Joachim
Will. According to F. C. Radke of Tecumseh, Nebraska, Will "stood with old Wiseman on the Missouri bluffs when a canoe
with two Indians came downstream.
Wiseman waited till they came within
range. He raised his gun, his old army
musket, and fired. One Indian fell into
the bottom of the canoe, the other pad-
dled frantically. The gun sounded again.
The canoe overturned, and floated empty
down the river."

Radke added that "many an Indian
canoe floated down the Missouri with
its passenger missing. . . . a shot rang
out of the woods when peaceful bands
were passing and the shots never
missed."

The Indians knew of Wiseman's hate
and tried to give him a wide berth. The
only shooting Wiseman himself ever admitted to was that of the wounded Indian
who said Wiseman had been his attacker.
Yet Wiseman's silence may not have
been as innocent as it seems, for this
kind of vigilante justice was forbidden
and, supposedly, had Wiseman admitted
to committing such deeds he would have
been prosecuted for murder. One thing
is certain, however—if Wiseman did indeed carry out his vendetta against the
Indian nation, it is unlikely, as long as
he himself did not admit it and no white
man accused him, that the community
would have raised much objection.

Mrs. Pearl Guy, a granddaughter of
the Wisemans, said in 1963 that she remembered her grandfather and that she
thought the "revenge stories" were "far-
fetched." But Judge Radke and others
persisted in maintaining the truth of
the embittered man's obsession. "Whenever he heard that there were Indians
in the vicinity he watched for them con-
stantly."

No one was ever sure which individuals
or which tribe were responsible for the
deaths of the Wiseman children. Wiseman himself maintained it was the Yankton and Santee Sioux, but the only concrete evidence concerning the deaths was
the confession of the two Indians who,
captured by the army, said that they had
killed a family in northeast Nebraska.
The Indians were executed, but no record
seems to exist of their names or tribes.

Addison Sheldon, former secretary of
the Nebraska Historical Society, was
particularly disturbed by this aspect of
the Wiseman legend:

"Cedar County citizens have told me
that Henson Wiseman carried his rifle
with him through the years; that he was
always ready at the sight of an Indian
to level the loaded rifle and fire. I am
not sure how absolutely true this tradition may be . . . . yet one can understand
the bitterness that ate into Henson Wiseman's heart. And it was not confined to
Indians. Wiseman never forgave the government for failing to protect his family when his family was all the more
vulnerable because he himself had volunteered to leave home to protect the
frontier."

AT THE AGE of seventy-seven, Wiseman still brooded on the events which
had changed his life. "If I had known the
Government [was] . . . , of savage warfare so ignorant, I would have sent my
family away when I left," he wrote.

Smouldering with anger and sorrow,
he asked the government for damages.
His claims were not exorbitant, nor were
they intended to make up for the loss of
his children. He simply wanted re-
imbursement for his stolen goods and for
the expenses he incurred in taking
Pheobe back east. His case was con-
vincing, for he had ridden away from his
family, certain that the military would
offer them protection.

He sent a bill to the United States
Congress, with a petition signed on his
behalf by two state governors and a
territorial governor. He was supported
by a Nebraska senator and a number of
citizens. He fought for over two decades
to have his claim honored, and died
finally at ninety-four, his efforts in vain.
His only harvest was bitterness—with
one exception. The government decided
not to brand him as a deserter when he
rode away that August day to find
out what had become of his family. He
was given a belated honorable discharge.
That was all. That, and the damages.

At seventy-seven Wiseman wrote "Now
to a candid world. If I should treat one
of my neighbors as I have been treated
by the government, I would have been
put out of sight long ago. . . . My family
was buried in blood, dirt and rags, like
so many dogs, their mother not able to
see them to their resting place. I received an honorable discharge from the
army, but not from dread of duty. Those
Indians stole from me; for four years
after all this, I was on my guard and
was shot at. I wore a Colts revolver
for five years night and day. . . ."

Pheobe lived to be eighty and, when
she died, was buried beside her children,
whose bodies had been moved to the
St. James cemetery. Henson Wiseman
died in 1912, and was laid beside them.

St. James itself is gone now. The log
cabin is gone too, and the clearing where
Wiseman lived, where his children died,
where Pheobe, in after years, cried out
in terrified dreams, and where Henson
himself carried his two guns and hated

the Indian nation and the U. S. government. This clearing is accessible still by
a neglected road. A rusting fence surrounds a monument, raised in 1927, which
announces to the wilderness that five
Wiseman children died on this spot. If
you stand there quietly, it seems you
can almost hear the woods inching closer,
feel the oaks and basswood closing in
tighter, almost feel the coldness of the
violence that was such a part of the
frontier.

In the neighboring hills—those tall,
old, green, unexpected hills of northeastern Nebraska—lie the bones of the
Indians who lived there before the
Wisemans, perhaps of those Indians who
murdered them. The summer rains wash
bones out of the ground on hilltops, and
farmers still find arrow heads when they
turn the furrows.

St. James and Wynot were the out-
posts to the Dakotas. The land is not,
in general, good for farming or grazing.
Many a settler's grave lies in clearings
like the Wiseman's, clearings growing
over, going back to the wilderness. Even
in the cemeteries, the stones tilt, the
weeds flourish, graves sink. And here, on
the edge of the Pa Sapa, the sacred land
of the Sioux, and the fringe of the Indian
Wars, nature seems determined to reclaim the land, and to erace the traces of
what transpired among these hills. The
coyotes howl here; the deer are coming
back. And the bones of the Wiseman
children, like the bones of the dead Sioux,
are going back to the dust that inflamed
them all to battle and to bloodshed. Just
the story of that complex and lonely
soldier, Henson Wiseman, lives on.

The Wiseman Massacre

Mystery, Myth Surround Ghastly 1863 Killings South Of Yankton

Robert F. Karolevitz, Press & Dakotan

While it was not a proud moment in U. S. history when 38 Santee Indians were hanged in Mankato, Minn., on Dec. 26, 1862, at least the mass executions brought to an uneasy end the so-called War of the Outbreak which had struck fear into the hearts of white settlers in Minnesota and Dakota.

At Yankton the hastily-built stockade — which had never been attacked — was eventually torn down, and farmers returned warily to their fields.

However, in the year that followed, wandering bands of young renegades continued to roam the area in the aftermath of the uprising.

On May 6 east of Yankton at J. B. Greenway's ferry crossing of the Jim River (near today's Fleeg's Riverside Road House), the murder of J. A. Jacobson by unidentified Indians inflamed local citizens. Word quickly reached the territorial capital that he was killed as he and Thomas W. Thompson were sleeping in their wagon. Awakened, Thompson ran for Greenway's cabin, but he was seriously wounded in the neck by an arrow. On May 12 the Weekly Dakotian editorialized:

"The scene of the late butchery by the Indians of the lamented Jacobson is but five miles from Yankton — one of the most populous settlements in Dakota — and directly on the main thoroughfare between us and Sioux City. No wonder our farmers feel insecure and seek the security of town every evening at nightfall. How much longer must this state of affairs continue?"

Territorial Secretary John Hutchinson was then serving as acting governor because a successor to Dr. William Jayne had not yet been appointed. Testily, he wrote to Brig. Gen. John Cook, commander of the First District of the Army's Department of the Northwest:

"SIR: On the 8th ultimo I made a requisition upon you for three companies of soldiers, to be stationed at different points in this Territory, to which you have never seen fit even to reply.

"I have now to make a second requisition for immediate protection. Last night Mr. Jacobson was killed by Indians at Grannays [sic] Ferry on James River, about four miles from this place and another man wounded. This must increase the alarm which has heretofore existed. The people are not secure in their homes, and we must have protection at once, or more lives will be lost and the Territory abandoned. I hope, General, you will give this sufficient consideration to act upon it, or give it at least a reply."

Whether or not Hutchinson's letter was responsible, on May 26 the Dakotian was able to report: "Eight hundred soldiers have passed through Yankton within the past week. ... This has the appearance of business." Immigration was seriously affected, though, and to counter the growing apprehension, the paper — on July 7 — said that the Indian problem was overblown.

Then, less than three weeks later, a more gruesome tragedy occurred some 15 miles or so southeast of Yankton on the Nebraska side of the Missouri. There are some conflicting reports of the incident, but here, generally, is the story.

In 1857 Henson and Phoebe Ann Wiseman settled with their then five children on their homestead some 3 1/2 miles from Old St. James, Neb. For five years the family fared well, and a fifth son — Loren — was born. When the Santee uprising occurred in 1862, a Home Guard was formed as Co. I of the 2nd Nebraska Cavalry, and Henson Wiseman enlisted, ostensibly to defend his and his neighbors' homes should the outbreak spread south of the Missouri.

However, the War Department planned a retaliatory move against the Sioux, and the 2nd Nebraska Cavalry became part of the expeditionary force under Gen. Alfred Sully. This, of course, included Wiseman, serving as a scout with his unit.

Before he left home, Henson apparently wanted his wife and five children (John, the oldest boy, was by then a soldier in the Union Army) to move into St. James where they would be safer. Phoebe refused, as she supposedly said jokingly that "there isn't an Indian within a thousand miles."

On July 21 she left her children — with son Arthur, 16, in charge — to go to Yankton to buy provisions. She walked to St. James, took the Ponca to Nebraska stage to Elm Grove across the river from the Dakota territorial capital and stayed the night with friends. In the morning she crossed the Missouri — probably by rowboat — to do her shopping.

It is likely that she stopped at the store of Downer T. Bramble, made her purchases and then returned home on July 23 on the same stage. When she arrived near nightfall after the long walk from St. James, she came upon a most ghastly scene. All five or her children (two of them were still barely alive) had been brutally assaulted by Indians. Three of them were already dead, and Hannar (or Hannah), the 14-year-old daughter, lived for five more days, and Loren, the 4-year-old son, died after 72 hours.

An obviously inaccurate and inflammatory account in volume 14 of the South Dakota Historical Collections, 1928, said that Hannar, erroneously noted as age 18, had an iron poker jammed down her throat, and "the youngest, a babe of a few months, was found baked to death in the oven." There were no infants in the family.

Probably more factual was the report that the house was plundered, a horse belonging to the Wisemans was stolen and several hives of bees were robbed of their honey.

Panic-stricken, Phoebe fled to St. James, but no one dared accompany her back to the homestead in the dark of night. It was the next day before several men (the Collections account called them soldiers) went to the Wiseman home to do what they could. When the news reached Sioux City, a military surgeon was sent to try to save the girl, but he was unsuccessful.

Two detachments of the Dakota Cavalry were ordered belatedly to pursue the culprits back across the Missouri and up the Jim River valley. The Collections report said that the attackers were led by a son of Inkpaduta (Scarlet Point), a Santee chieftain who had participated in a massacre at Spirit Lake, Iowa, in 1857 during which 42 settlers were killed. Just who was involved in the Wiseman raid were never identified, and their trail was lost.

Whether it is true or not, Henson Wiseman apparently learned of the tragedy at Crow Creek where he was stationed when several Indians arrived at the agency with plunder from a raid. Among the spoils displayed were shoes which he recognized as those of his daughter.

Yanktonians, of course, were shocked when they learned of the killings. What it did was to incite an even greater anti-Indian attitude among territorial settlers — an attitude which 145 years later still thwarts the cause of reconciliation.

Photo shows Henson Wiseman in his late years.

Henson Wiseman

The Frontiersman's Revenge

By Joan Burney

Until the massacre, Henson Wiseman might have been described as a typical frontiersman. He might have lived out his life, trading peacefully along the Missouri River, and be remembered now only by his descendants.

But fate was to decree otherwise, and Henson Wiseman has become a legend; made so by a tragedy so ugly one cannot stand on the peaceful knoll where it occurred, and where the Wiseman Memorial now stands, without sensing the horror.

In this instance, a white family suffered; but survivors at Wounded Knee could tell their own horror stories as the white man and Indian fought for the rich prairieland.

Born in West Virginia in 1817, Wiseman married Phoebe Ann Cross in 1838. They migrated to Iowa, where Henson worked at carpentering. While in Iowa the couple had eight children, two of whom died and were buried there.

In 1857, the Wisemans along with about 10 other families ("a total of perhaps 50 people") became the first settlers in Cedar County, Nebraska.

Wiseman selected a picturesque plot of land in the northeastern part of the county under the "squatters law." He built a cabin which consisted of two separate log rooms connected by a hall, all under one roof.

The site was chosen with care. The cabin was located in a wooded area, on a knoll where two ravines met, near a stream. The wooded area provided ample cord wood and abounded with deer and wild turkey. Wiseman was noted for his ability as a marksman. The family cleared land for a garden, and Wiseman discovered and captured a hive of bees.

All of which enabled Wiseman to trade extensively with the 30 or 40 steamboats which churned up the muddy Missouri River in the spring and summer, providing them with fowl, honey, venison, catfish, garden produce and cord wood.

In 1859, they lost one of their boys (the first natural death in Cedar County). That same year, another son was born, so their family again numbered six. The eldest son, John, joined the Army and left home to fight in the Civil War.

About this time bloody Indian battles were taking place all along the frontier, although the settling of Cedar County had been accomplished peacefully with trading contracts with the Sioux and Ponca Indians.

o o o

But as the red man and the white man perpetrated increasingly cruel acts of violence against one another in the bloody border warfare of 1862, 1863, and 1864, the families in Northeast Nebraska realized that their settlements represented advance picket posts against hostile Indians.

Speaking at the dedication of the Wiseman Memorial in 1927, Addison E. Sheldon, secretary of the Nebraska Historical Society, detailed what happened:

"A great council of Indian tribes of the plains and mountains was held in 1863 on Horse Creek in Nebraska, and after days of counseling and feasting, the tomahawk and scalping knife were sharpened and war signals passed swiftly from the Red River of the north to the distant Rio Grande, making the next two years one continuous battle line of red warriors across 2,000 miles of frontiers."

The Wiseman children were to be caught in the middle of that battle field.

o o o

Because of the Indian uprisings, Nebraska's scattered frontiersmen were called upon to organize a new regiment. Thinking they were to protect their own families, they responded. Wiseman himself had not been on good terms with the Indians, according to historians. They both feared and hated him.

So Henson Wiseman enlisted on Oct. 28, 1862. The original enlistment record describes him as follows: "Age, 44; Height, 6 ft.; Complexion, dark; Eyes, dark; Hair, black; Born, W. Virginia; Occupation, farmer; enlisted at Dakota City by Captain John Taffee. Term of enlistment, nine months."

Wiseman trained at Dakota City, as did the other 50 citizens who had enlisted from the county's population which had grown to about 275. They were in Company 1, 2nd Nebraska Cavalry. In June, 1863, the company was ordered into Dakota to take part in Sully's campaign against the hostile Sioux, thus depriving Northeast Nebraska of many of its best men.

But Wiseman was sure that back-up troops would come in to defend his home. He wrote: "I told my wife and children we were going, and they all cried and said, 'The Indians will kill us if we stay here and you leave us.' I told them that other soldiers would come as soon as we were gone. Now my children were put to a wretched death by the ignorance of the government; (that was the last I ever saw of them) anyone there of knowledge would say the Indians would come in behind . . ."

Apparently Phoebe Wiseman overcame her fears, however, and when her husband urged her to move to old St. James for safety, she refused.

On July 21, Phoebe set out to get supplies, leaving behind her five children ranging in age from 5 to near 16. Phoebe, two months pregnant, walked the three miles down the ravine to St. James, rode the stage mail to Elm Grove — across from Yankton — where she spent the night, crossed to Yankton on the ferry for a day's shopping, returned to Elm Grove for another night and then caught the stage back to St. James.

Members of the George Hall family, where she spent the night, remembered asking her if she wasn't afraid to leave her family because of the Indians. She replied, "There isn't an Indian within 1,000 miles."

(Henson was to write later: "My wife was not at home at this time . . . or she too would have shared the same fate . . .")

Phoebe was delayed in St. James by a violent summer storm, and was encouraged to spend the night. But she said she was anxious to get to her children, and started home. It was about dusk.

As she neared her cabin, she stopped a minute to rest, wondering why the children and the dogs hadn't come to greet her.

As she approached the yard she saw books and papers strewn all over and blood smeared on the door. She rushed along the west side of the cabin and stumbled over the body of her 8-year-old son, dead. Looking fearfully through the window, in a state we can only imagine, she saw Arthur and An-

drew lying on the floor. Arthur, almost 16 years old, was badly beaten, and it was obvious that he had put up a terrible struggle. Phoebe rushed into the house, but thinking she saw a live Indian in the hall she fled in panic to find help.

Henson Wiseman wrote: "She fled, leaving all roads and going through high weeds and brush all dripping wet with rain . . . what kind of feelings for a female in her condition! Is this protection, I ask?"

Phoebe got to St. James, but the nine men there dared not risk going back until dawn, for fear of ambush. When they arrived at the scene the next morning, taking a circuitous route to avoid the wooded areas, they found a sight "that would freeze the blood of anyone."

o o o

In Henson Wiseman's own words, they "found three dead and two nearly so. The youngest boy, aged 5 years could tell 'the Indians scared him.' It was all he ever said; he was stabbed under the left arm and lived three days. The girl, (Hannar) 15 years of age . . . bore savage infamy . . . a cartridge put in her mouth, was set on fire, tearing out her teeth . . . she lived five days; never spoke a word but looked wildly around to anyone that came in her sight. The other three were dead; one boy, aged 8 years, was found outdoors shot through with a ball and three buck-shot; all the rest were in the house. The next boy, aged 13 years, was stabbed twice in the left side. The oldest boy had his hand and arms all broken and mashed, his gun, clutched in his hands, showed an over-hand fight and was empty. There were four guns in the house; two the Indians took and two they left."

Arthur had, by all evidence, put up a heroic fight. One historical account conjectured that the guns left behind are evidence that two Indians were killed; "An Indian will never take a gun with which an Indian has been killed."

This same author gives a possible motive for the massacre, writing that "an Indian boy named Chaska (three years older than Arthur) belonging to the Yankton Sioux told William Gyte that a family in the neighborhood would be killed about the time corn was in the roasting ear. Arthur Wiseman had whipped Chaska in a personal encounter."

Wiseman, himself, 200 miles away, did not learn of the tragedy for a month. According to him, many letters were written, but they were kept from him to keep down a mutiny in the regiment.

When he did learn about it, ("Indians gave the news at the Crow Agency, wearing my wife's shoes . . ."), he took off without leave and rode home like a wild man, stopping only at Fort Randall, where they tried

to arrest him as a deserter until they heard his story. Then "they gave me all I wanted."

He reached St. James to find his wife, nearly crazed with grief, had left. Sick and exhausted, he went to his blood-soaked cabin. It was said "a terrible change came over him."

Wiseman went in search of his wife. He found her coming home. "She wailed and cried and tried to tell me her grief but could not, and it was a year before she could tell it all."

On March 8, Phoebe bore a son "restless and under great trouble." Wiseman took her East in the hope she would find some peace.

They returned to Cedar County after a year, however, and remained for the rest of their lives, having another daughter, Laura.

When Henson was 77 he wrote the account of the massacre quoted here. He wrote it for the purpose of appealing to Congress to settle the claim he'd had in for many years—not for the loss of his children—but for the substantial financial loss he endured.

o o o

He was almost as bitter toward the government as he was toward the Indians, writing:

"Now to a candid world. If I should treat one of my neighbors as I have been treated by the government, I would have been put out of sight long ago. Thirty-two years have passed. I did not live on government land nor on the Indians' hunting ground. But forced in old age to hard labor; my life made miserable, my family buried in blood, dirt and rags, like so many dogs; their mother not able to see them at their resting place. I received an *honorable discharge from the Army but not from dread of duty.* Those Indians stole from me for four years after all this. I was on guard and shot at."

There was much talk about Henson Wiseman's vendetta against the red man. By his own account "I wore a Colt's revolver for five years, night and day, and during the day I spent the time working for my bread, and at night examining the country for miles around to be sure that no Indians would be in waiting at dawn of day, as I knew their intentions were to kill me."

o o o

There are those who think it was the other way around. Addison Sheldon acknowledged this in his dedication address: "Cedar County citizens have told me that Henson Wiseman carried his rifle with him through the years; that he was always ready at the sight of an Indian to level the loaded rifle and fire."

Other accounts say, "He shot Indians on sight thereafter, always leaving their bodies in attitudes of prayer" and, "Many an Indian canoe floated down the Missouri with its passenger missing."

Top photo, the ravine that Phoebe Wiseman followed to St. James. Above, Phoebe as an older woman. Right, tombstone rests near cabin site.

Mrs. Pearl Guy, granddaughter of Henson Wiseman, believes these stories are exaggerated. She remembers Grandpa and Grandma Wiseman as being just like other folks. When Phoebe died at 80, Mrs. Guy's family went to live with Grandpa Wiseman, and she remembers him as a mellow old man who loved to visit with his grandchildren.

"If he used his weapon it was to scare the birds who were bothering his bees," according to Mrs. Guy.

Sheldon was not "absolutely sure how true the tradition may be" and he "cannot commend it." Said Sheldon: "For it must always be said, after doing full justice to the dying and the suffering of the white frontiersman, that the Indian has suffered as much injustice at the hands of the white man as the white man has at the hands of the red man."

There was never any proof of which tribe participated in the massacre.

Historian Sheldon doubted that it was either of the local tribes, because of their long, unblemished record of cooperation and friendliness. Two Indians were eventually shot for it by Indian Agent Burleigh's scouts, but there is no record as to their tribe.

Henson Wiseman died in 1912, his claim never settled with the government. Some say he died an old man embittered with hatred of the Indians and the government. Many would understand that, considering his loss. But his granddaughter says he died a gentle old man, full of love. Perhaps the truth lies somewhere in between.

Nobody, however, would deny the truth of one of Sheldon's statements at the memorial dedication.

"War makes beasts out of men," he said.

And little children suffer.

Wiseman Massacre

In 1862, about 50 of the citizens of Cedar County joined Company I, of the Second Nebraska Cavalry, raised for the purpose of defending the frontier settlements against Indians. Some members were John Andre, Henry Klopping, Ernest and August Ferber, William Guite, Henry Morton, Henson Wiseman and Moses H. Deming. Deming was a First Lieutenant. This regiment went to Dakota in 1863 to join General Sully's command. During the absence of Wiseman, a party of Yankton and Santee Sioux attacked and killed his five children, who were at home alone. Despite his wife's fears of being left alone with the children, Henson Wiseman answered the call of men to fight warring Indian tribes in the Dakotas. Wiseman requested his wife and five children (the oldest son, John, was serving in the Federal army at the time), to move to old St. James for greater safety, but she refused to leave her home.

On the 21st day of July, 1863, Mrs. Wiseman walked to St. James, took the Ponca to Niobrara Stage to Elm Grove where she spent the night with friends. Elm Grove was the name of a Post Office about a mile above the present site of Strahmburg, (Green Island). When asked if she did not fear to leave the children on account of the Indians, she replied that there was not an Indian within 1,000 miles. The next morning she crossed to Yankton, made her purchases and returned to Elm Grove, staying the night with other friends. With thoughts of urgency to get back home to St. James, she left by the same stage on the 23rd. On her walk home from Old St. James, passing the Jones' house, Mrs. Jones fixed supper for her and tried to get her to stay the night. She was determined to go. She walked the distance (3 to 4 miles) to her home, carrying her purchases with her, arriving about dark. She found the house in great confusion and her five children (ages 4-16 years) had been brutally murdered and mutilated by some Yankton and Santee Sioux Indians. Seeing what a terrible struggle for life had taken place, she fled panic stricken, taking the roundabout route up the west ravine to Old St. James. Nine men were there but no one dared go to the scene that night. The next morning, after the terrible news reached the East Bow, several men from the area went directly to the scene. What they saw

"would freeze the blood". Three of the children had been killed outright, the four-year-old boy lived three days and the 14-year-old daughter lived 5 days. The bodies were taken to Old St. James and laid out in the general store. Their bodies were prepared and buried in Old St. James, until the Spring of 1893. Located on a hill, at the southern edge of Wynot, is the Wynot City Cemetery (originally called St. James Cemetery, then Bow Valley Cemetery). It was laid out in 1874. Here the five Wiseman children were reburied in 1893 in a plot beside their Mother and Father.

Found in an early recollection of tidbits in an old paper, is the story of Mary Connery, an early pioneer. She and her husband homesteaded not too far from the Wiseman's. In those days the Indians were quite numerous, and although, peaceful for the most part, went on the warpath occasionally. They often made raids on the white settlements and farmhouses, taking things to eat and other useful articles. During one of these raids, which resulted in the Wiseman family massacre, Mrs. Connery was captured. The Indians came to the Wiseman home while Mr. and Mrs. Wiseman were away, having left at home several children. The Indians took what they wanted from the house and then went to the barn and started away with a valuable cow. The oldest boy came out with a shotgun and tried to scare the Indians away. Enraged, they butchered all the children and started on the warpath. This massacre occurred near St, James and the whole surrounding country as far south as Martinsburg was overran and terrorized. Mrs. Connery after being bound and gagged, was left for a time and succeeded in freeing herself from her bonds and made her escape.

Mr. Wiseman vowed vengeance on the Indians and for years laid in ambush, shooting every Indian who came within range of his rifle. He was such a good shot and killed so many that the Indians became deathly afraid of him and they would go miles around in order to escape his sure shot.

Near the spot where this tragedy took place, a monument for the memory of the Wiseman Massacre was erected in 1926 by the Home Culture Club. They were assisted with funds collected from all over the county. Surrounding the area is an iron picket fence. This fence formerly enclosed the Lewis E. Jones burial plot in the Wynot City Cemetery. It was donated for use at this area.

Wausa, tucked off in the southeast corner of Knox County, can more easily identify with Hartington of Cedar County than with most of its sister villages in Knox. Seven years before the Indian massacre of the Brabenec children on the Pischelville bottom (see pages 45-53), a somewhat similar tragedy occurred near Hartington.
The Hartington History Book tells the story:

WISEMAN MASSACRE

Henson Wiseman, along with about a dozen other settlers of the county, had joined an army unit that was fighting marauding Indians in Dakota Territory. On July 21, 1863, about a month after he left his wife and five children, Mrs. Wiseman left the farm and went to do some shopping in Yankton. While she was gone Indians attacked the children, who had been at home alone. It is not known whether the children became frightened and shot at the Indians to provoke the attack, or whether it was the outright massacre that it appeared to be.

All five of the children died, three of them instantly, and the other two within the next five days. A seven-foot stone monument has been erected to the memory of the children. Standing upon a knoll where the Wiseman log cabin had been located, it gives the names and ages of the victims: Arthur, 16; Hannar, 14; Andrew, 9; William, 8; Loren, 4.

There were other Indian scares within the next few years but none of them amounted to anything. By far the greatest threat to these early settlers were the elements of nature: bitter cold winters, blizzards, drought, flood and grasshoppers. In the early 1860s settlement was relatively slow, but the Becker, Lammers, Suing, Kohls, Wieseler, Kollars, Goeden, Kleinschmit, Haberman, Zavadil, Klug, Wubben, Arens and other families moved into the northern part of the county and staked out their claims.

VIOLENCE BEGETS VIOLENCE

One month after the Wiseman massacre a military post was set up at St. James to protect the settlers, with detachments stationed at Niobrara, Dakota City, Ponca and St. Helena. Later that same year Company B of the Seventh Iowa Cavalry stationed at Niobrara robbed a band of unoffending Poncas near Niobrara, killing four of their females. No big deal, the episode was quickly forgotten, whereas the Wiseman children became the martyrs of northeast Nebraska.

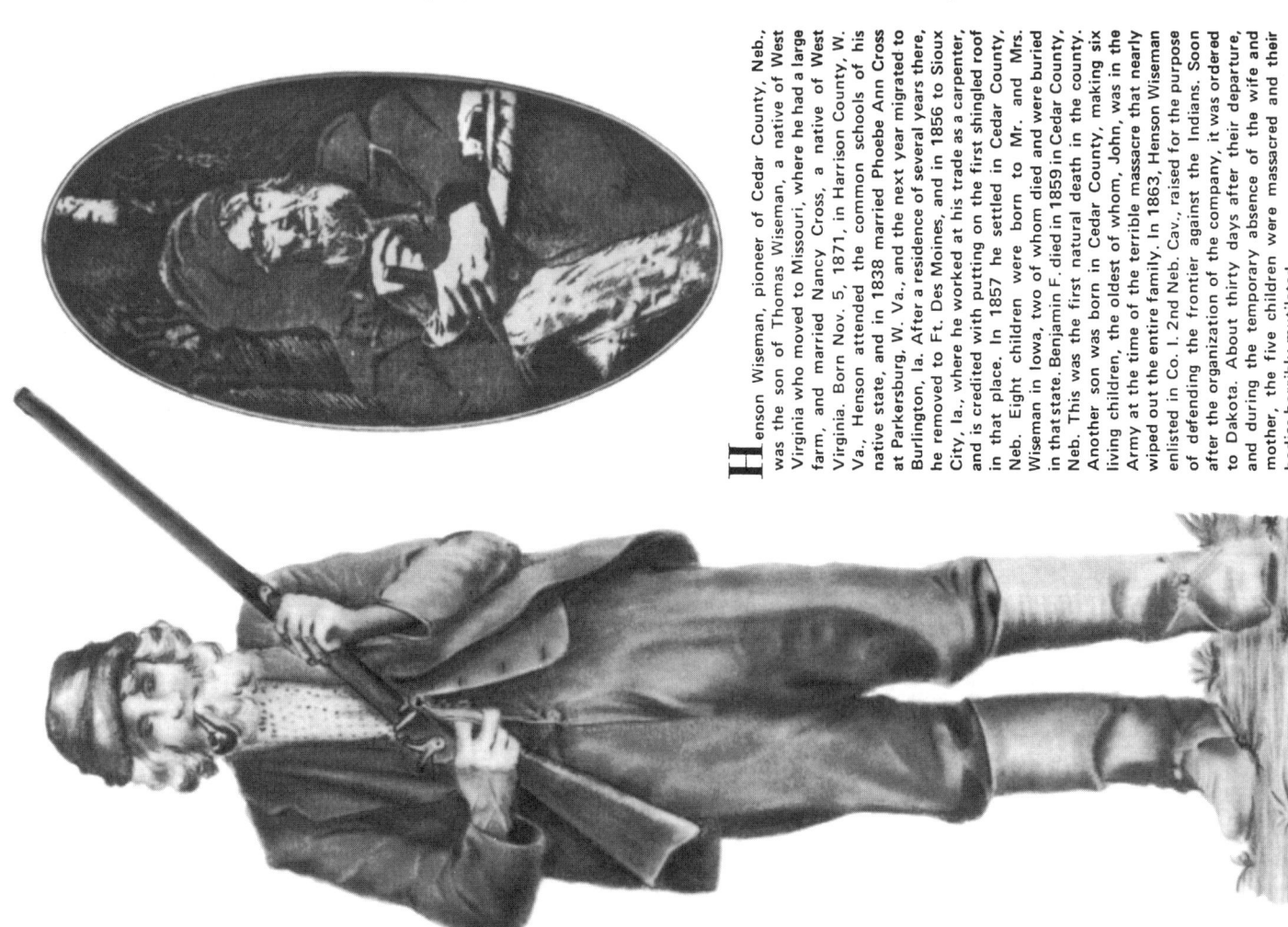

Henson Wiseman, pioneer of Cedar County, Neb., was the son of Thomas Wiseman, a native of West Virginia who moved to Missouri, where he had a large farm, and married Nancy Cross, a native of West Virginia. Born Nov. 5, 1871, in Harrison County, W. Va., Henson attended the common schools of his native state, and in 1838 married Phoebe Ann Cross at Parkersburg, W. Va., and the next year migrated to Burlington, Ia. After a residence of several years there, he removed to Ft. Des Moines, and in 1856 to Sioux City, Ia., where he worked at his trade as a carpenter, and is credited with putting on the first shingled roof in that place. In 1857 he settled in Cedar County, Neb. Eight children were born to Mr. and Mrs. Wiseman in Iowa, two of whom died and were buried in that state. Benjamin F. died in 1859 in Cedar County, Neb. This was the first natural death in the county. Another son was born in Cedar County, making six living children, the oldest of whom, John, was in the Army at the time of the terrible massacre that nearly wiped out the entire family. In 1863, Henson Wiseman enlisted in Co. I, 2nd Neb. Cav., raised for the purpose of defending the frontier against the Indians. Soon after the organization of the company, it was ordered to Dakota. About thirty days after their departure, and during the temporary absence of the wife and mother, the five children were massacred and their bodies horribly mutilated.

The original Wiseman log house, with Wiseman's relatives

According to the "History of Cedar County, Nebraska":

Then pregnant and needing supplies, Mrs. Phoebe Wiseman walked to St. James on July 21, 1863, and took a stage to Elm Grove — across from Yankton, South Dakota — where she spent the night. The next morning she crossed to Yankton by ferry, made her purchases and returned to Elm Grove. Then on the 23rd she returned to St. James. Despite a thunderstorm, she walked three or four miles to her home. Arriving there about dark, she found the house in great confusion and that her five children, ages 4 to 16, had been brutally mutilated by Sioux Indians.

Upon seeing what a terrible struggle for life had taken place, she fled panic stricken, taking a circuitous route up the west ravine to Old St. James. No one dared to go to the scene that night. The next morning when several men went to the scene what they saw "would freeze your blood". They found three children dead, and two nearly so. The youngest, Loren, age four, was sitting on his own bed with his arm around the post. He asked for water, saying, "Indians scared me." Stabbed under the left arm, he died three days later. The 14-yr-old daughter, Hannar, had been raped, and died of her injuries five days later.

The bodies were taken to the Old St. James for burial where they remained until the spring of 1893, when they were moved to the St. James Cemetery (now known as Wynot City Cemetery) and buried in the family plot beside their parents.

A CARTRIDGE EXPLODED IN HER MOUTH . . . ?

Most of the accounts of the Wiseman massacre, including the one above written by Twila Anderson, are pocked with inconsistencies. One story tells of Mrs. Phoebe Wiseman finding two of her dead sons lying next to the body of an unconscious Indian. Supposedly drunk, the Indian was gone when neighbors came to investigate. We are also told that "a cartridge had been put in Hannar's mouth, and lit, tearing out her front teeth." Anyone familiar with ballistics would have trouble figuring out how such a procedure could have been accomplished.

The photo shows the Wisemans' log cabin where the children were slaughtered. A monument, erected in 1926, now stands on that spot. Wiseman had used the cabin as his headquarters while working as a "woodhawk," cutting wood and selling it to passing river steamers.

As will be seen below, the Bentz murder and the Wiseman family are making quite a stir in Cedar County. It will be remembered that several weeks ago the *Pioneer* spoke of the Wiseman family being deserving of Congressional aid after the murder of their five children by the hands of Indians. This editorial was copied extensively in the State press and in the press of Iowa and Dakota. About two weeks after the appearance of that article, we received the following anonymous note written on a postal card:

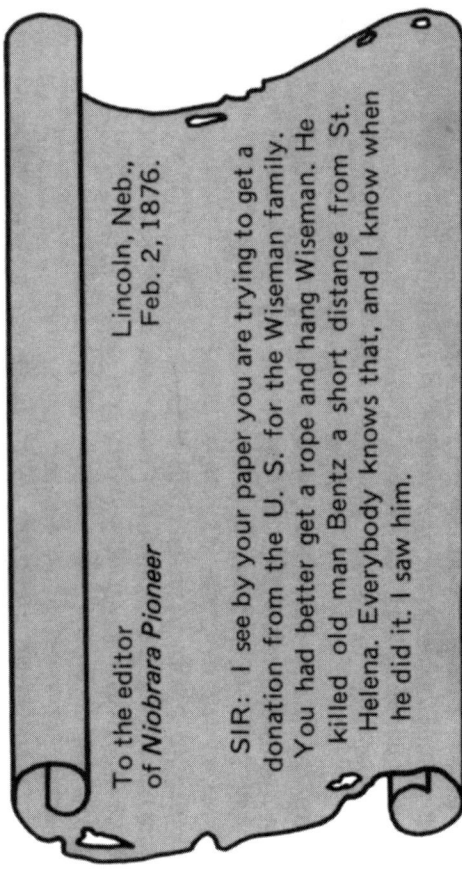

Lincoln, Neb.,
Feb. 2, 1876.

To the editor
of *Niobrara Pioneer*

SIR: I see by your paper you are trying to get a donation from the U. S. for the Wiseman family. You had better get a rope and hang Wiseman. He killed old man Bentz a short distance from St. Helena. Everybody knows that, and I know when he did it. I saw him.

Mr. Wiseman is now trying to discover the author of the above. And, to further the progress of the investigation, we have forwarded the anonymous communication to P.C. Nissen, Esq., who is now in possession of Doctor Bentz's papers. The following is from the *Cedar County Advocate*:

The murder of Doctor Bentz is supposed to have been committed on the 14th day of April, 1864, in a cabin he then occupied situated on a hill between St. Helena and Green Island. Doctor Bentz, the victim, was at that time living alone in his cabin, which had a door in the south end facing the road, and but one window on the west side. It is thought he was killed sometime during Thursday, April 14, 1864, but his death was not discovered until the following Saturday when Henry Felber, Sr., of this place, was on his way from Yankton and decided

From Danny Liska's Book "River Rat Town"

Too often Indians were blamed for crimes they didn't commit. And somehow we just can't accept the record that the Brabenec children were killed by Indians. If they were, why didn't the Indians take their scalps—and that of Mrs. Brabenec? Who saw the Indians that massacred the Wiseman children? Why weren't they scalped?

The Santee Sioux with whom I discussed the Wiseman and Brabenec tragedies vehemently rejected the notion that the Santee — or any other tribe, could possibly have been responsible for these killings. No warrior band would stoop to killing defenseless children, they argued — and any Indian who would so demean himself would automatically be ostracized from the tribe. However, the carrying off of white children was a common practice — because Indians, by nature, had an exaggerated fondness for children, and would, whenever possible, kidnap white kids and give them to the older folks to raise.

What sort of a man was Henson Wiseman? Had he acquired enemies who were capable of taking revenge by killing his offspring? Could someone, perhaps a non-Indian, have raped Wiseman's daughter and then killed the others when they came to her aid? Was Wiseman capable of committing murder? We were somewhat shocked by the inferences of the following article which appeared in the March 9, 1876, issue of the Niobrara Pioneer suggesting that, 9 months after the Wiseman children were killed, Wiseman may have "killed old man Bentz a short distance from St. Helena."

MURDER!
The Bentz Murder of Twelve Years Ago Revived

Niobrara Pioneer.

Mar. 9, 1876:

A Postal card of an Anonymous Writer to the *Pioneer*.

What will Become of it is Yet to be Determined, but Time will Tell.

Burleigh claimed his Yankton Scouts executed the Indian killers

In 1859 Yankton Indian agent Walter Burleigh (see** p. 275) purportedly submitted a little-known and long-lost report relating how his Yankton Indian Scouts, led by Walking Elk, had overtaken and executed a renegade Indian war party on the Vermillion. According to Burleigh's communique, before their execution the ringleaders confessed to having killed 10 whites in Minnesota — and the five Wiseman children in Nebraska. With Burleigh being the shyster he was, and considering the fact that he organized the Yankton Scouts to improve his flagging image (of screwing the Indians and accumulating some 10,000 acres of Bon Homme County's most fertile farmland), any serious historian would have to take his "long-lost communique" with a grain of salt.

Always sly and ruthless, Burleigh cheated the Scouts out of the $10,000 they had coming in wages. He also ended up with Charles F. Picotte's 640 acres of Yankton City property (see marginal notes p. 276); and then sent the penniless half-breed back to die among his people.

By the 1870s Burleigh had melted away from the political scene and become a colorful riverboat master who owned the Black Hills paddleboat which was competing against the Coulson line in hauling freight between Sioux City and the upper Missouri. In the fall of 1876 Burleigh entered into a downriver race from Fort Pierre to Yankton against the fastest boat on the Missouri, the E.H. Durfee, and won.

The two steamboats were still neck and neck when they anchored for the night at Bon Homme Island where the E.H. Durfee's wily master, Bill Massey, bought up all available firewood from the local woodhawks. Undaunted, Capt. Burleigh ordered his cargo of salted pork tossed into the furnances, and with this the Black Hills, "with black smoke pouring out of her funnels, every timber in the boat creaking in protest and the smell of frying bacon wafting over the Missouri behind her," shot into the lead five miles above Yankton and won the race.

to go to Bentz's house to rest and visit a few moments with the doctor, who was an intimate friend. After knocking at the door and receiving no answer, he pushed it open and entered the cabin. Finding the old man lying on the floor, Felber spoke to him, thinking that perhaps he was sick; but, upon approaching nearer, he was horrified to find the floor covered with blood and the doctor dead. He immediately went to St. Helena to report what he had seen at the cabin. A number of men went for the premises, and upon entering they found the victim lying in his own gore, a pistol-ball hole in the back of his head and his brains scattered over the floor. Upon a small table, at which it is supposed the doctor was sitting at the time he was shot, was found a partly-written letter directed to his son, then in the army of Southern Nebraska — but killed a short time afterward by Indians while scouting. The last word in the letter was not finished, and it is thought he was killed while in the act of writing that word. The letter was dated April 14, which probably establishes the date of Bentz's murder.

No doubt the writer of the card, mailed at Lincoln, who says he "saw Wiseman shoot Bentz," wants to stop the government from giving the Wisemans an appropriation, and also to underline the fact that, on the day of the murder, Wiseman had been asked to go to Bentz's home and deliver some sacks which somebody had given him. These sacks were later found outside the door of Bentz's cabin — and Wiseman claims that, after knocking at the door and receiving no reply, he dropped the sacks where they were found and resumed his journey home.

If one seriously considers the possibility that Wiseman killed Doctor Bentz — then we would have to go a step farther and look for a reason. That reason night have been that Wiseman had suspected Bentz was the one who had raped his daughter — and the real author of the "Wiseman Massacre." ■

Also from Danny Liska's book River Rat Town

Although the relatively friendly Ponca had been moved across the Niobrara after their 1858 treaty with the government, Indian scares persisted, and news of the bloodbath caused by rampaging Santee Sioux in Minnesota obliged the government to organize the Second Nebraska Cavalry for the sole purpose of defending the settlers from marauding Indians. However, in June 1863, this outfit departed to chase Indians in Dakota Territory, and in their absence five white children of the Wiseman family were massacred near St. James, Cedar County. Controversy surrounds these alleged Indian atrocities, with Inkapaduta's band of renegade Wahepekute Sioux being blamed for the Wiseman deaths, and a roaming band of Teton Sioux for the killing the Brabenec children on the Pischelville bottom.

St James Cedar County Nebraska
September the 13th 1874
I enclose you $40 H Wiseman
Dear son I onley send you a fiew tines
is for a direction take the Des morne
Valey Road to Boonesburough
then to the Missouri valey junction
then to Sioux City and vermillion
and stop at the station calld
meckling on the Dakota Suthren
Railroad) you are then just five
miles from my house there is a
man by the name of Stuart that
carries the mail across the river
for St james and newill bring
you a cross rite at once john tailor
is the Station keeper

john come assoon as you can and
as cheap as posible money is hard
to comeat those hardtimes
H Wiseman to john G Wiseman
Rockwood pro Ill

Letter from Henson to John, sending money and directions to get home.

The Wiseman

Homestead

And

Land

History of Wiseman Homestead

By: Ray Guy & Laura (Bensen) Bruce, 1992

Henson Wiseman homesteaded after the massacre located in Precinct 6, Township 32, Range 3E in Section 8 @ 17, northeast of Wynot, Nebraska. After the massacre in July, 1863 Phoebe and Henson roamed the land. After visiting back in West Virginia they came back to Nebraska and settled in Precinct 6 about 1865.

Henson built a dugout in the valley west of the present house. Then he built a log cabin down the hill from the dugout. Next they built closer to the river in the bank with an eastern exposure. Phoebe died in 1901.

Their daughter Laura Wiseman married Nels Christian Lawson March 8, 1887. When they were first married they lived a mile and three quarters east of the Wiseman homestead on the south side of the road.

Then Nels and Laura built a wood frame house in front of the house in the bank about 1908 or 1909. The south part of this house is where Henson lived. Nels and Laura lived in the north part. Henson died February 19, 1912. After that the house was rearranged and Henson's room became the kitchen.

Nels and Laura Lawson had a house built in Wynot, Nebraska by Frank Konegi in 1918. Nels and Laura moved in the fall of 1918 to Wynot.

Ernest Brown bought the Wiseman place but later lost it.

In the spring of 1926 Pearl (Lawson) and Willard Guy bought the Wiseman homestead and moved there from west of Obert, Nebraska. At that time they had two sons. Vernon was five and Ray about two. Their other son Harold was born April 4, 1927 on their tenth anniversary.

In 1953 Pearl and Willard Guy moved to Hartington, Nebraska. Their son Harold was married to Teresa Lammers June 30, 1953. Harold and Teresa moved to the Wiseman homestead. They farmed until 1954 or 1955 and then moved to Yankton, South Dakota.

Pearl and Willard moved back to the Wiseman homestead. In 1962 they retired and moved to Wynot, Nebraska. Their oldest son Vernon and wife Ilith (Flom) moved to the Wiseman homestead from southwest of Hartington, Nebraska. They inherited the homestead in 1974.

The hill part of the Wiseman homestead was sold by Vernon in 1985 to the State of Nebraska and became a Wildlife Management area. The building site and river front was sold to James Lewon also in 1985. Lewon was remodeling the house and on January 24, 1986 the house burned to the ground. Lewon then moved a modular home to the site and lived there the same year.

These pictures were taken at the Wiseman Wildlife Area. The surrounding hill land is where the Wiseman's lived. This area is northwest of the monument. Visitors are welcome and encouraged to explore this beautiful area. The wildlife area does not include all of the land that Henson once owned. His last homestead and river front land is located right here. Much of the river front land is gone now because of the river eating it away through the years. The Wiseman home that was on the property burned down in 1986, during a remodeling project.

The original
St. James

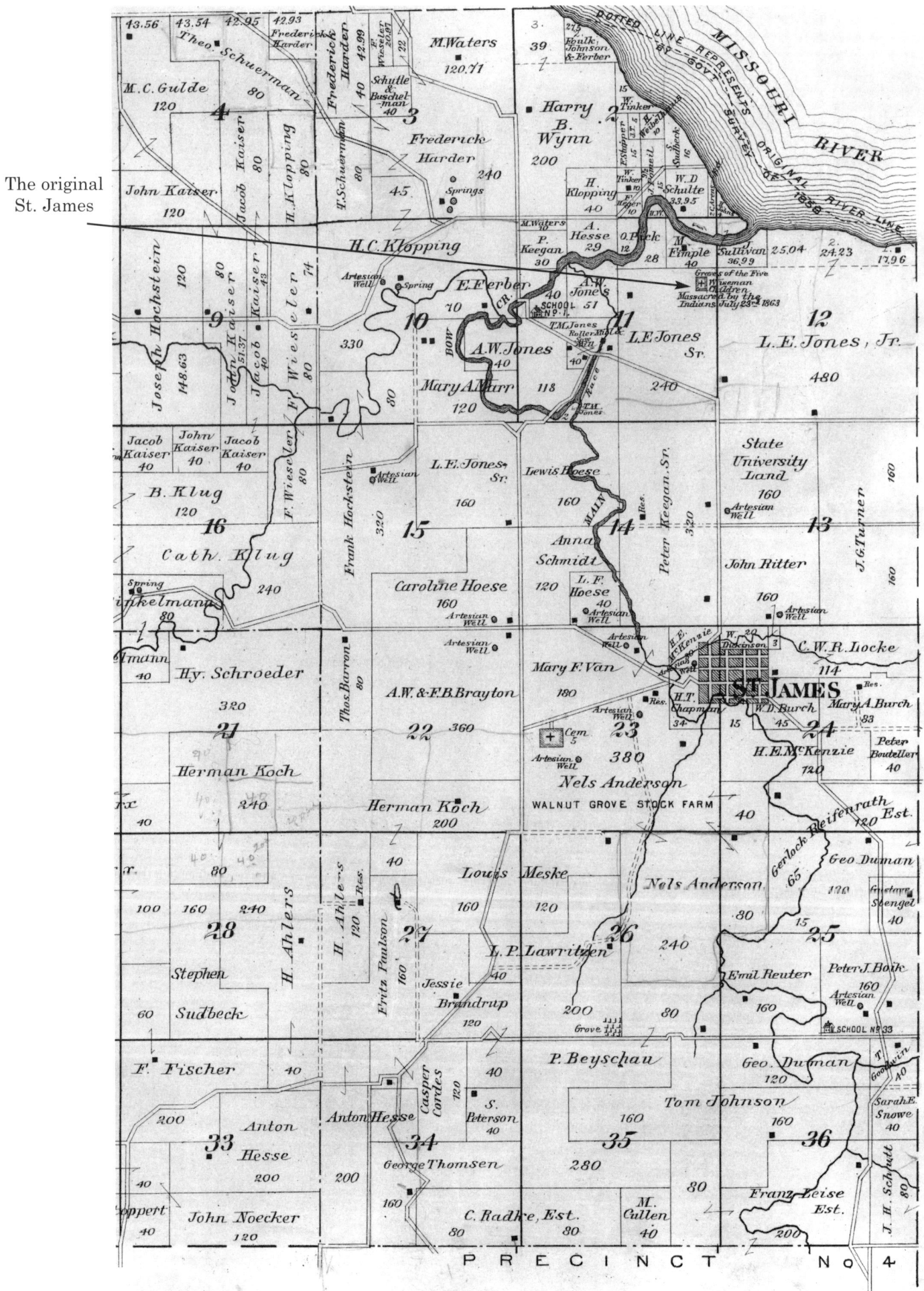

Plat book of Cedar County Nebraska. NorthWest Publishing Company 1899

Scale 2 Inches to the Mile.

Rattle Snake Road

Wiseman Place
after Massacre
and Wildlife
Management Area

Brookey
Bottom Park

Wiseman
Monument

DOTTED LINE REPRESENTS
BY GOVERNMENT ORIGINAL SURVEY OF RIVER LINE OF 1855

MISSOURI

ORIGINAL RIVER

J. E. Jones Jr.
55.06

Wm Smith
51.76   47.63

John Ritter
38   40   53

J. H. Schutt
40

A. W. Jones
40   67

H. Wibel-haus
40

S. Stevens
40

30

Cloche
22.5

Artesian Well

R. Brewer
60

Henson Wiseman
80

PIONEER HOMESTEAD

Henson Wiseman
70

Brewer
H. P. McKenzie
Haymond Brewer

John Ritter

J. T. Witthouse

Hoese
50.97

P. B. 10
Wm 10

J. C. Dawson 10

SCHOOL No. 27

Mikkelson & Iverson
40.19   31.81   29.96   28.61
Artes Well

Saw Mill
S. Boyles
40

37.62

H. E. McKenzie
40

80

Gerloch Reifen-rath
40

Wm Arens
40

F. Sappen 20
J. Homel

Wisner
W. Marc

L. Arens
40

L. Uhing
40

J. H. Felber
40

Artesian Well

Henson Wiseman

Peter Lund
320

Artesian Well

Theo. Beste
300

PROPOSED

Artesian Well

15
160

G. Reifen
40

18

A. C. College

36.88

36.12

C. W. R. Locke
80

35.38

Albert Erdenberger
40

E. Ferber
40

McKinney L. & I. Co.
160

16
Artesian Well

Theo. Beste
280

Spring
34.78

F. Burch
40

Sam'l Swetland
160

College & Colpoys
160

Nels Anderson
160

Nels Anderson
40

40

F. C. Shepard
120

S. Wahlman
40

M. Koch
40

Theo. Beste
320

Fred
120

B. Townsend
80

34.42

19

Mary A. Burch
80

B. Townsend
40   40   40

P. H. Peterson
80

Peter J. Boik
160

21

N. Anderson
200

P. J. Boik
40

John Gallagher
80

P. C. Shephard
80

22

33.88

Peter Boutteller
40

33.42

Geo Duman
33.05

Gustave Stengel
120

Henry Morten
200

120

40

John J. Roche
200

John J. Roche
320

28
George H. Eastman
320

320

27
280

W. H. Stephen-son
40

John F. Anderson
40

E. R. Nichols
40

John Ko

W. Kon
40

30

Wm Willoughby
32.15

Peter J. Boik
80

T. Goodwin
40

H. E. McKenzie
80

O. Swan
80

29

Wm Gowery
120

Carrie Wiggins
32.39   40

Henry Thoene
80

Sam'l Allen Est.
160

H. E. McKenzie
160

B. Winter-ringer
40

Lewis Betts
200

Wm Smith
80

C. Thompson

SCHOOL No. 60

AMES SPRING

33.17

Mary Thoene
160

31

E. W. Weis
80

32

E. G. Helpel
160

Morris & Gould
80

33

W. N. Rousch
80

K. P. Jansen
200

34
120

J. C. Da
200

Sarah E. Snowe

33.95   40

J. H. Schutt
34.73   40

J. H. Bourbon
40

A. J. Chorn
40   80

B. S. Shop

E. Warner
240

PRECINCT N° 4